Blessed
Are the
Unlikelies

Other books by Philip W. Dunham

Blinded by the Light: The Anatomy of Apostasy

Sure Salvation: You Can Know You Have Eternal Life

PHILIP W. DUNHAM

Blessed Are the Unlikelies

Pacific Press® Publishing Association
Nampa, Idaho
Oshawa, Ontario, Canada
www.pacificpress.com

Cover design by Steve Lanto
Cover illustration by Darrel Tank
Inside design by Aaron Troia

The author assumes full responsibility for the accuracy of all facts and quotations as cited in this book.

Chapter 1 of this book, "Manasseh, King of the Unlikelies" (with allowances for additions and revisions) originally appeared in Philip Dunham's book with Maylan Schurch, *Blinded by the Light: The Anatomy of Apostasy* (Hagerstown, Md.: Review and Herald® Publishing Association, 2001), 167–175.

You can obtain additional copies of this book by calling toll-free 1-800-765-6955 or by visiting http://www.adventistbookcenter.com.

Library of Congress Cataloging-in-Publication Data:

Dunham, Philip W. (Philip Winfield), 1928-
  Blessed are the unlikelies : God values the most improbable people /
Philip W. Dunham.
    p. cm.
  ISBN 13: 978-0-8163-2427-9 (pbk.)
  ISBN 10: 0-8163-2427-1 (pbk.)
  1. Rogues and vagabonds in the Bible. 2. Rogues and vagabonds—Biography. 3. Salvation—Biblical teaching. I. Title.
  BS579.R6D86 2010
  220.9'2—dc22
                                                                          2010029056

10 11 12 13 14 • 5 4 3 2 1

Dedication

I dedicate this book to all those believing, kingdom-bound souls
who wonder if indeed they will ever make it home,
and to our wonderful God,
who made the unlikeliest sacrifice
for every single being ever born on this planet.

Contents

Introduction

For some time, I have been thinking about people in the Bible who seem to be unlikely candidates for the kingdom. People such as Lot, Ishmael, Aaron, Rahab, Barak, Gideon, Jephthah, Samson, Manasseh, Nebuchadnezzar, and the disciples (early on). All these people are going to be in heaven, safe and saved. None of them, however, come to our minds when we think of giants of faith we want to emulate. In fact, many of them leave us wondering how they made it at all. But they did make it. They will be in the kingdom. Abraham, Isaac, and Jacob will be there—and so will Barak, Jephthah, and Samson. What kind of salvation equity is this? Has God no standards about the kinds of people He'll let in through the gates into the city?

Deep down, all of us are quite aware of our shortcomings, our secret evils, and our faults and failings. They all loom large in our thinking and often make us despair as to our ever being in the kingdom. Am I all that I should be? No! Do I always please God like Jesus did? No! Am I still struggling with sins that should have been out of my life long ago? Uh, yes! Satan, the accuser in chief, presses these matters on our minds and our consciences; he whips us with them, making us wonder if we'll ever make it to the home of the pure and the blessed. However, when we become aware of "saints" such as those I listed above, hope arrives; and we pick ourselves up, dust ourselves off, straighten our shoulders, and press onward and upward with a new spring in our steps. If Samson can make it to heaven, so can I. If Manasseh can be there, I can too.

Seeing the grace of God in how He's given eternal life to people who don't seem to have been very spiritual, gives us hope that we can win that prize too. Not that we should conclude that if they're good enough to be saved, we're good enough too. Rather, we should praise God because of

His mercy, His love, His forgiveness, and the grace that He pours down on this sick, sinful, lost planet.

When we consider the "unlikelies," it becomes marvelously evident that God is in the saving business, not the losing business. He is "not willing that any should perish" (2 Peter 3:9). Why, that can make even a conservative Seventh-day Adventist say "amen" right out loud!

Chapter 1
Manasseh, King of the Unlikelies

In Old Testament times, when little Hebrew kids were learning to write, they scratched their alphabets on pieces of broken pottery. I wonder if they also made up little poems about people. If so, the verse about wicked King Manasseh might have gone something like this:

Manasseh was a little boy when he became the king.
He never ever thought of God, but did his wicked thing.

I've heard that nursery rhymes often taunt the politics of an era, so it's possible that the kids who lived during Manasseh's reign made up rhymes like this one.

Whatever the case, Manasseh's extreme wickedness did give rise to a lot of frustrated irony, even among kids. You see, Manasseh wasn't just your common, average, ordinary sinner. Instead, he was a Luciferian monster—a super-wicked, evil man. Some people inspire me because of how good they are. Others, like Manasseh, give me a kind of backhanded inspiration because he was such a wretched human specimen for most of his life and he still found salvation.

That's the point of his story: if God could love Manasseh and keep on loving him, and if He could save Manasseh, *then He can love and save anybody*. But don't take my word for it. Check it out in 2 Kings 21 and 2 Chronicles 33. (You have to look at both or you won't get the whole story.)

Before the change

The only good thing I can find about the first part of Manasseh's life was that his father was Hezekiah and his mother was Hephzibah—according to

Jewish tradition, the prophet Isaiah's daughter. So Manasseh came from good stock. Too bad he wasn't a chip off the old block, because Hezekiah was a great and a good king—one of Judah's three best. Yet daddy's boy Manasseh vied with Jeroboam and Ahab for the "honor" of being one of the three worst kings God's people ever had.

Though Manasseh's biography is one of the shorter ones in the Bible, his reign was one of the longest: fifty-five years. In that biography, you'll find a chillingly gruesome catalog of evils. In fact, the sins he led his people to commit were worse than the sins of the heathen nations that the Lord had driven out of the land! And not only did Manasseh worship the gods of the Canaanites, but he also searched far and wide for new deities to reverence. One historian wrote, "Every faith was tolerated but the old faith of Israel."[1]

Manasseh not only abandoned this faith, but he also forbade it. In its place he instituted hellish tortures, such as causing children to "pass through the fire" (2 Kings 21:6). Some scholars believe that this was a euphemism for placing babies as offerings on the red-hot arms of an internally heated metal idol. Another historian asserts that not only did Manasseh put Baal's female counterpart in the Most Holy Place of the temple, but he then proceeded to remove the ark from that room, which had been created for it.[2]

I don't care who you are, if you let go of God, there's no telling how far into evil you'll descend. That makes your being in God's kingdom increasingly unlikely. So, at some point, God has to try something drastic to get your attention. "Because Manasseh king of Judah has done these abominations (he has acted more wickedly than all the Amorites who were before him, and has also made Judah sin with his idols), therefore thus says the Lord God of Israel: 'Behold, I am bringing such calamity upon Jerusalem and Judah, that whoever hears of it, both his ears will tingle' " (2 Kings 21:11, 12).

In the book *Prophets and Kings,* Ellen White says that Manasseh had a way of "silencing every voice of disapproval."[3] One of the voices he may have silenced was that of Isaiah, whom, according to tradition, he had sawed in half. Are you getting the picture of Manasseh?

Even Manasseh's name seems eerily prophetic. It means "one who forgets." And he did forget—forget the example of his parents, the teachings of his God, and the fact that he was accountable for his actions. Do you remember that during the reign of Josiah, Manasseh's grandson, Josiah's servants found some scrolls that had been lost—scrolls that contained God's law? Guess when they were lost. During Manasseh's reign.

Manasseh reminds me of the evil character Aaron in act 5, scene 1, of Shakespeare's *Titus Andronicus*. Aaron says,

> Tut, I have done a thousand dreadful things
> As willingly as one would kill a fly,
> And nothing grieves me heartily indeed
> But that I cannot do ten thousand more.[4]

During most of Manasseh's life, he could have said the same thing. What a man! He's the king of all the unlikely candidates for the kingdom. But, praise God, his story didn't end while he was filling that role.

After the change

"The LORD spoke to Manasseh and his people, but they would not listen," writes the author of Chronicles sadly. "Therefore the LORD brought upon them the captains of the army of the king of Assyria, who took Manasseh with hooks, bound him with bronze fetters, and carried him off to Babylon" (2 Chronicles 33:10, 11).

Payback time, right? In that era, payback was common practice. When you'd captured an important prisoner, you'd pierce his nose or his upper or lower lip, put a hook through the hole, and attach a thong to the hook. Then you'd lead the once-proud person along like an animal—subjecting him to utter subjugation, subservience, and humiliation.

Esarhaddon, the king of Assyria, lists King Manasseh by name in his military annals. He indicates that Manasseh was one of twenty-two monarchs whom he had conquered and humiliated. Esarhaddon says that he made these rulers—Manasseh included—haul building materials "under terrible difficulties, to Nineveh," where Esarhaddon was rebuilding his royal palace.[5]

"Even if he deserved it," someone says, "what a way to end up!"

But it wasn't an end—it was a beginning! It was this terrible experience that turned Manasseh around. "When he was in affliction," the inspired biographer reports, "he implored the LORD his God, and humbled himself greatly before the God of his fathers, and prayed to Him" (verses 12, 13).

Why did it take so long for Manasseh to catch on? Why did he have to waste more than half his life? Why did he have to hit bottom first?

I guess you could say that he was like the mule the farmer had to hit with a two-by-four to get its attention. But, really, those questions are pointless and irrelevant because Manasseh did humble himself.

He did turn to the Lord.

He did beg God for help.

And he did return to the God of his father and mother, the God of Israel— the God of the universe. Second Chronicles 33:13–20 tells the rest of his story and gives proof of his conversion.

A man like Manasseh—converted! What a miracle! What a change! Couldn't he have been dubbed "Mr. Unlikely" at one point, when to think of him ever being in the kingdom of God was such a stretch? And couldn't he have qualified as the spiritual comeback kid of that century?

But as great as the ending of his story is, it has an element of sadness too. Manasseh couldn't undo all the evil he had done. When he returned to the Lord, he couldn't bring with him all the one-time believers he had led astray. Unfortunately, his son Amon was one of those who didn't make it back (verses 22, 23).

Beyond this, the scars from his past wicked life remained, and scars sometimes serve to remind us of the pit we've been in. Manasseh's grandson might have triggered a reminder if, while sitting on his lap, he asked, "Grandpa, what are those scars on your lips?"

However, by faith in the God who is always faithful and who loved him, Manasseh burned the bridges to his old life. Jude 23 speaks of those who will be just barely snatched out of the fire, who will just barely make it—the "singed but saved." Manasseh fits that category.

Lessons to learn

A wicked apostate—changed. Amazing!

But it's just as amazing that God *didn't* change. Throughout the sordid reign of this flagrantly erring human, through all his forgetting, his rebellion, and his dragging so many down with him, God kept on loving him just as much as He had when Manasseh was Hezekiah's baby boy. This, you see, is the most mind-boggling part of Manasseh's story. The import and the impact of the story of a man like Manasseh is what it reveals about a God like our God! I'm very grateful that Manasseh turned around, but the most beautiful part of his story is that *God didn't turn His back on him!*

Ellen White said that in this story, "The Lord gives us an instance of the way in which He works." Though He "has often spoken to His people in warning and reproof," He has "revealed Himself in mercy, love, and kindness" and "has not left His backsliding people" but "has borne long with them" with "compassionate love." "We have reason to offer thanksgiving to God that He has not taken His Spirit from those who have refused to walk in His way."[6]

"Tongue cannot utter it," she says.

> Pen cannot portray it. You may meditate upon it every day of your life; you may search the Scriptures diligently in order to understand it; you may summon every power and capability that God has given you, in the endeavor to comprehend the love and compassion of the heavenly Father; and yet there is an infinity beyond. You may study that love for ages; yet you can never fully comprehend the length and the breadth, the depth and the height, of the love of God in giving His Son to die for the world. Eternity itself can never fully reveal it.[7]

What lesson, then, does Manasseh's story teach us? Have your fling, and then after you're all flung out, turn to God? Play around with your idols first, and then, when you tire of the games and stop them, God will still be around? See how long you can play probation roulette and still make it home free?

None of the above.

But there are many love lessons we can learn from God's dealings with Manasseh. "No soul is ever finally deserted of God, given up to his own ways, so long as there is any hope of his salvation. 'Man turns from God, not God from him.' "[8]

God's love isn't fickle. It is said that the preacher Charles Spurgeon visited a farmer one day and noticed that his barn had a weathervane on it that said, "God is Love."

"My good man," Spurgeon asked, "do you mean to tell me that God's love is as changeable as the wind?"

"No sir," the farmer replied calmly. "I'm saying that God's love is the same whichever way the wind blows."

God's love isn't doled out tit for tat to keep the heavenly accounting books balanced.

There is no degree of wickedness—none—that is beyond the reach of God's love.

God, with His unfathomable love, is more anxious to forgive us than we are to sin.

"There is nothing in all creation that will ever be able to separate us from the love of God which is ours through Christ Jesus our Lord" (Romans 8:39, TEV).

God loves you, backslider.

God loves you, sinner.

God loves you, Laodicean.

God loves you, wavering, undecided one.

God loves you, weak, struggling, trying to be a Christian.

God loves you, doubting, fearful, anxious heart.

God loves you, falling, failing, stumbling one.

God loves you, most unlikely one.

You see, the great controversy is not just about Sabbath versus Sunday. Primarily, it's about the character of God. It's about whether you believe the devil's propaganda about God or whether you've discovered the greatest truth in the universe: *God is love!* There's nothing you can do to make Him love you more, and there's nothing you can do to make Him love you less.

When you discover this, and when it really sinks in, you'll do anything for Him. And as you continue to make this discovery, you'll do everything for Him.

His lip throbbing, a humiliated Manasseh discovered this at the lowest point in his life, and he repented. "In his suffering he became humble, turned to the LORD his God, and begged him for help. God accepted Manasseh's prayer and answered it by letting him go back to Jerusalem and rule again. This convinced Manasseh that the LORD was God" (2 Chronicles 33:12, 13, TEV).

The point is that if God loved a man like Manasseh, maybe there's a remote chance for me. If God heard and answered Manasseh's desperate prayer, maybe He'll hear and answer some prayers of mine. God forgave Manasseh, so maybe He'll forgive me again. God was so patient with Manasseh—maybe He'll be patient with me. If Manasseh was such an unlikely candidate for the kingdom and yet was blessed, maybe I can be in the kingdom too.

In fact, if God loves us like He loved Manasseh, there's no maybe about it!

1. William Smith, *Dr. William Smith's Dictionary of the Bible,* eds. Horatio Balch Hackett and Ezra Abbott (Boston: Houghton Mifflin, 1888), s.v. "Manasseh."

2. Ibid.

3. Ellen G. White, *Prophets and Kings* (Mountain View, Calif.: Pacific Press® Publishing Association, 1943), 382.

4. William Shakespeare, *Titus Andronicus,* ed. Jonathan Bate, 3rd Arden Shakespeare ed. (London: Thomson Learning, 2006), 5.1.141–144. References are to act, scene, and lines.

5. James B. Pritchard, ed., *Ancient Near Eastern Texts Relating to the Old Testament,* 2nd ed. (Princeton, N.J.: Princeton University Press, 1955), 291.

6. Ellen G. White, Ellen G. White Comments in *The Seventh-day Adventist Bible Commentary,* ed. Francis D. Nichol (Washington, D.C.: Review and Herald, 1980), 3:1132.

7. Ellen G. White, *Testimonies for the Church* (Mountain View, Calif.: Pacific Press® Publishing Association, 1948), 5:740.

8. Ellen G. White, *Thoughts From the Mount of Blessing* (Mountain View, Calif.: Pacific Press®, 1956), 93.

Questions for Reflection and Discussion

1. Did God send disasters upon Manasseh and his people to force Manasseh's repentance?

2. What do Manasseh's decades of rebellion of the worst kind say about the "unpardonable sin"?

3. God was pretty quick, pretty ready, to accept Manasseh as His child and return his kingdom to him. What would indicate whether or not He did so prematurely?

4. How can we tell the story of Manasseh without misconstruing it, so as to give people license to live any way they wish, knowing that God is willing to take them back as He did Manasseh?

5. Comment on this statement from Ellen White's *The Desire of Ages:* "Our Redeemer has opened the way so that the most sinful, the most needy, the most oppressed and despised, may find access to the Father. All may have a home in the mansions which Jesus has gone to prepare."[*]

6. What makes us sure that Manasseh will be in the kingdom?

---

[*]Ellen G. White, *The Desire of Ages* (Mountain View, Calif.: Pacific Press®, 1940), 113.

Chapter 2
Righteous Lot?

There's little written about Lot. And no other person in the Bible is named Lot, so when you see the name *Lot,* you're not likely to be confused as to who is being spoken of. Even the meaning of the name is uncertain.

Lot is mentioned thirty times in the Old Testament. Twenty-seven of those references are in the book of Genesis, and thirteen of them—nearly half of the times he's mentioned in the Old Testament—are in Genesis 19 alone. This is the chapter that chronicles the destruction of Sodom and Gomorrah. And Lot is spoken of four times in the New Testament, once by Peter and three times by Jesus. Each of these four times he's linked with Sodom and its wickedness. The story of Lot, then, is inextricably connected to the wickedness, the judgment, and the destruction of the inhabitants of Sodom and Gomorrah—people who outsinned even the love, mercy, and forbearance of God. People who chose to give themselves over to extreme godlessness. Lot and his daughters were the only people who survived it all.

Lot is mentioned first in Genesis 11:27, and this verse simply relates his genealogy. Lot's grandfather was Terah, his father was Haran, and his uncle was Abram—not a bad family tree. Lot's father died early on, while the family still lived in Ur of the Chaldeans, which explains why the destinies of Lot and Abraham, nephew and uncle, were linked closely together in the new, promised land of Canaan. We don't know much about Lot's father, Haran, but we do know a lot about his uncle Abram, and, of course, we know Abram was a good person to be connected to.

A lot of good

Lot must have had some desire to benefit from the promise God made to his uncle Abram. He didn't have to move away from Ur. He didn't have to face all the uncertainty that the trip involved. He must have had confidence that the Lord would fulfill His promise to his uncle Abram and that Abram would possess the land of Canaan. Lot must have held Abram in high esteem, and he must have trusted that God guided Abram through dreams and visions. It would seem that he must have felt that his earthly interests and his heavenly hopes were bound up with his uncle. And so, because of Lot's good points, Scripture says, "Terah took his son Abram and his grandson Lot, the son of Haran, and his daughter-in-law Sarai, his son Abram's wife, and they went out with them from Ur of the Chaldeans to go to the land of Canaan" (Genesis 11:31). The book *Patriarchs and Prophets* adds, "Besides Sarah, the wife of Abraham, *only Lot,* the son of Haran [who was] long since dead, chose to share the patriarch's pilgrim life."[1] Let's give Lot some points for turning his back on Ur and turning his face toward Canaan.

The apostle Peter gives us further insights into the kind of man Lot was. "God rescued Lot, *a man who had his approval* ["righteous Lot," NKJV]. Lot was distressed ["sickened," "greatly troubled," "shocked," "driven nearly out of his mind," as other Bible versions have it] by the lifestyle of people who had no principles and lived in sexual freedom. Although *he was a man who had God's approval,* he lived among the people of Sodom and Gomorrah. Each day was like torture to him as he saw and heard the immoral things that people did" (2 Peter 2:7, 8, GOD'S WORD; emphasis added).

Lot must have had some kind of enlightenment, some kind of spiritual awareness and sensitivity, for him to be so turned off by the blatant wickedness. That says he had some good qualities.

One of Lot's impressive character traits was his unquestioning hospitality. We don't know, for we aren't told, whether he learned this from his father, from Abraham, or whether it was just part of the culture. Perhaps, it was a blend of these factors. But Lot's hospitality was very apparent—Scripture makes this clear: "Two angels came to Sodom in the evening, and Lot was sitting in the gate of Sodom. When Lot saw them, he rose to meet them, and *he bowed himself with his face toward the ground.* [Quite a bit beyond a casual "Hey, why don't you come by for supper?"] And he said, 'Here now, my lords, please turn in to your servant's house and spend the night, and wash your feet; then you may rise early and go on your way' " (Genesis 19:1, 2; emphasis added). They remonstrated; but verse 3 says, "He insisted strongly; so they turned in to him and entered his house. Then he made them *a feast,* and baked unleavened bread, and they ate" (emphasis added).

Paul would have given Lot high marks, because he lists hospitality among the spiritual gifts that come from God and are of the Spirit (see Romans 12:13). Paul also lists hospitality as one of the characteristics required of those who hold high offices in the church (Titus 1:8). Surely, the Lord Himself was pleased that Lot had this positive, spiritual trait. So, there can be no question that Lot had a number of good character traits. There is no discernible evidence that he had a settled determination to live at cross-purposes with the will of God or that he was in open rebellion against God. To the contrary, there is evidence that it was in his heart to obey God and, indeed, that he put forth efforts to this end.

But Lot had glaring faults. We mustn't gloss over these imperfections, so we'll examine them. We don't have to look far to find the evidence that he was less than perfect.

A selfish choice

We find the first indication of Lot's negative characteristics—aside from the fact that he was born into the human family—in Genesis 13. That chapter says the herdsmen of Abraham and those of Lot started quarreling—or worse—because their flocks and herds were so large that the land couldn't sustain them all. It was obvious that they'd have to separate and move to different areas.

Abraham was the head of the family and should have had his preference as to where he would live and what grazing land he wanted for his flocks. But, characteristically, he let Lot choose first. In the Contemporary English Version, Genesis 13:8, 9 reads, "Abram said to Lot, 'We are close relatives. We shouldn't argue, and our men shouldn't be fighting one another. There is plenty of land for you to choose from. Let's separate. If you go north, I'll go south; if you go south, I'll go north.' " That's indeed like Abraham! Maybe Lot was acting characteristically, too, when he chose first without respecting his uncle's rights. The New Living Translation continues the story this way: "Lot took a long look at the fertile plains of the Jordan Valley in the direction of Zoar. The whole area was well watered everywhere, like the garden of the LORD or the beautiful land of Egypt. (This was before the LORD had destroyed Sodom and Gomorrah.) Lot chose that land for himself—the

Jordan Valley to the east of them. He went there with his flocks and servants and parted company with his uncle Abram" (verses 10, 11).

Did Lot know what he was doing when he "pitched his tent toward Sodom" (verse 12, KJV)? The inspired record doesn't answer that question. But Lot did know what he saw. And the book *Patriarchs and Prophets* describes what he saw.

> Fairest among the cities of the Jordan Valley was Sodom, set in a plain which was "as the garden of the Lord" in its fertility and beauty. Here the luxuriant vegetation of the tropics flourished. Here was the home of the palm tree, the olive, and the vine; and flowers shed their fragrance throughout the year. Rich harvests clothed the fields, and flocks and herds covered the encircling hills. Art and commerce contributed to enrich the proud city of the plain. The treasures of the East adorned her palaces, and the caravans of the desert brought their stores of precious things to supply her marts of trade. With little thought or labor, every want of life could be supplied, and the whole year seemed one round of festivity.[2]

I can imagine Lot saying, "Thanks a lot, Uncle Abram. If it's OK with you, I think I'll choose the area around Sodom."

That's a tad bit greedy, Lot! It shows the contrast between his character and Abraham's. Ellen White mentions that when Lot and his family were taken captive by Chedorlaomer and his allies, Abraham immediately formed an army to rescue his loved ones because "he had cherished no unkind memory of Lot's ingratitude"[3]—that is, of Lot having chosen the best of the land.

Not only was Abraham generous, he also knew about the "cities of the plain" (verse 12, KJV) and how wicked the inhabitants were. Lot also must have known something of what he was getting into and that his family and their eternal welfare would be in jeopardy, but it seems this didn't figure large in the choice he made. Someone starkly summarized the seriousness of Lot's greedy choice in this brief sentence: "Lot thinking to get paradise, found hell."[4] And still another wrote, "Lot has fallen into the very vortex of vice and blasphemy."[5]

Scripture says, "The men of Sodom were exceedingly wicked and sinful against the LORD" (Genesis 13:13). Matthew Henry enlarged this thought by saying, "Though all are sinners, yet some are greater sinners than others. The men of Sodom were sinners of the first magnitude, *sinners before the Lord,* that is, impudent daring sinners; they were so to a proverb." He then adds this comment: "Filthy Sodomites dwell in a city, in a fruitful plain, while faithful Abram and his pious family dwell in tents on the barren mountains."[6] Another illustration that life isn't fair.

Ellen White draws the lesson from this: "Like Lot, many see their children ruined, and barely save their own souls."[7] Something happens to us when we constantly behold wickedness, when our senses are overwhelmed by an unremitting bombardment of sights and sounds of evil. And so it was that Lot, living in the capitol of vice, experienced his faith growing dim. So dulled were his senses that Ellen White says, "He did not realize the terrible necessity for God's judgments to put a check on sin."[8]

What had happened to Lot's ability to discern between good and evil? Was he thinking, *I know, Lord, that these people do a lot of bad things, but they are actually good people.* Apparently, he had become blind to the enormity of the sins committed by the sinners in Sodom.

Interestingly, *Patriarchs and Prophets* comments that Abraham knew that "familiarity with evil would insensibly corrupt the principles."[9] Lot, however, seemed not to know this—or if he did, he had stifled the thought.

Righteous Lot?

Lot's hospitality led him into an egregious act. He invited the two visitors who came to Sodom to spend the night in his home. That night, the men of the city came and pounded on his door demanding, "Where are the men who came to you tonight? Bring them out to us that *we may know them carnally*" (Genesis 19:5; emphasis added).

Lot's response is exceedingly difficult to understand. "Please, my brethren, do not do so wickedly! See now, I have two daughters who have not known a man; please, let me bring them out to you, and you may do to them as you wish; only do nothing to these men" (verses 7, 8).

This is the "righteous Lot"? Willing to give his daughters to a sex-crazed mob so "you may do to them as you wish"? Is this spiritual enlightenment? Is this representative of spiritual growth? Are we looking at the fruit of the Spirit in Lot's life? Unthinkable!

Anyway, the two angels made that unnecessary by blinding the mob. Then they warned Lot that God was about to destroy the whole area, including the cities of Sodom and Gomorrah, because of the sinfulness of the people who lived there; they told him to warn his sons and daughters and their spouses that they all must leave the area posthaste.

It isn't clear if Lot had sons nor how many daughters he had. But we have to wonder how Lot's choice of Sodom as a place to raise his family and how his "example" of godly living influenced them. Genesis 19:14 says, "So Lot went out and spoke to his sons-in-law, who had married his daughters, and said, 'Get up, get out of this place; for the LORD will destroy this city!' But to his sons-in-law he seemed to be joking." However many children he might have had, only two made it out of the city of destruction.

We see through another window into Lot's soul when we read that the angels—and there is good reason to believe that one of them was Jesus Himself—virtually had to drag him out of Sodom. Surely, he knew they were celestial beings. Surely, he knew that the destruction of Sodom was imminent. And yet Genesis 19:15 says, "The angels *urged Lot to hurry,* saying, 'Arise, take your wife and your two daughters who are here, lest you be consumed in the punishment of the city' " (emphasis added). Then the angels led Lot and his family outside the house and told them to escape for their lives to the mountains (verses 16, 17).

And still Lot was hesitant. He tried to bargain with the heavenly visitants. "Then Lot said to them, 'Please, no, my lords! Indeed now, your servant has found favor in your sight, and you have increased your mercy which you have shown me by saving my life [well, yes, Lot!]; but I cannot escape to the mountains, lest some evil overtake *me* and *I* die' " (verses 18, 19; emphasis added). Lot spoke in the first person singular. He was still thinking primarily of himself. Should he not have said, "Lest some evil overtake *us* and *we* die"?

Lot didn't want to go to a rural area—to the mountains. He suggested the angel let him go to a little city called Zoar, and the angel acceded to that request. But the angel still had to say, "Hurry, escape there. For I cannot do anything until you arrive there" (verse 22). In fact, verse 16 tells us, "*While he lingered,* the men [angels] took hold of his hand, his wife's hand, and the hands of his two daughters, the LORD being merciful to him, and they brought him out and set him outside the city." When the whole place was going to be turned into a raging furnace of destruction, what was the hesitancy about? What was there about the angels' warnings—that the Lord had sent them to destroy the cities— that Lot and his family didn't understand? Why did they linger?

The book *Patriarchs and Prophets* contains a terribly incriminating statement about Lot: "If Lot himself had manifested no hesitancy . . . his wife also would have made her escape. . . . His example would have saved her from the sin that sealed her doom."[10] Might we also reach this conclusion about the effect his example had on the rest of his children?

The saddest part of the story of "righteous Lot" is recounted in Genesis 19:30–36. I'll let the New Living Translation paint the picture.

Afterward Lot left Zoar because he was afraid of the people there, and he went to live in a cave in the mountains with his two daughters. One day the older daughter said to her sister, "There isn't a man anywhere in this entire area for us to marry. And our father will soon be too old to have children. Come, let's get him drunk with wine, and then we will sleep with him. That way we will preserve our family line through our father."

So that night they got him drunk, and the older daughter went in and slept with her father. He was unaware of her lying down or getting up again.

The next morning the older daughter said to her younger sister, "I slept with our father last night. Let's get him drunk with wine again tonight, and you go in and sleep with him. That way our family line will be preserved." So that night they got him drunk again, and the younger daughter went in and slept with him. As before, he was unaware of her lying down or getting up again.

So both of Lot's daughters became pregnant by their father.

Ellen White wrote, "The curse of Sodom followed him even here [to Zoar]. The sinful conduct of his daughters was the result of the evil associations of that vile place. Its moral corruption had become so interwoven with their character that *they could not distinguish between good and evil.*"[11]

Lot's prospects of making it to heaven aren't looking very good, are they?

Righteous Lot!

But wait! We must turn again to the inspired Word and look with wonder and amazement at how God regards this unlikely candidate for the kingdom of heaven. Second Peter 2:7, 8 says that God "delivered *righteous*

Lot, who was oppressed by the filthy conduct of the wicked (for that *righteous* man, dwelling among them, tormented his *righteous* soul from day to day by seeing and hearing their lawless deeds)" (emphasis added). In these two verses, we see that the "good heaven's keeping" seal of approval has been placed on Lot. Please consider the following points.

- The apostle Peter wrote his epistles some sixteen hundred years after Moses wrote about Lot in Genesis. Wouldn't what Peter wrote— that Lot was righteous—have to be the last word about him?
- The Bible does speak of other people as righteous (e.g., Abraham, Zacharias, and Elizabeth), but none so emphatically as it does Lot. It calls him "righteous" three times within two consecutive verses. And surely Inspiration wouldn't have repeatedly characterized Lot as righteous if he wasn't going to be in the kingdom.
- Doesn't Isaiah 26, Israel's kingdom song, declare in verse 2, "Open the gates, that the righteous nation which keeps the truth may enter in"? Is not righteousness a key entrance requirement—or *the* key entrance requirement for the kingdom? Wouldn't it follow then that righteous Lot will be in the kingdom?
- Isn't it likely that Christ Himself visited Lot in Sodom?
- Didn't Lot put himself under the guardianship of the heavenly visitants?
- Wasn't Lot delivered, saved from destruction, by his faith and obedience?
- Didn't Ellen White write of him: "Though Lot had become a dweller in Sodom, he did not partake in the iniquity of its inhabitants"?[12]
- Didn't Lot hold fast to his worship of God?

A good man, a good start, a good finish, a good record overall, but a human for sure, made mistakes for sure. Without question a sinner—involved in some very unspiritual, unseemly things. Not exactly a faith hero or a member of the spiritual Hall of Fame. But if the inspired Word calls someone "righteous," that person's life record must be commendable.

It seems that the story of Lot is written for the encouragement of those of us who live in the foul miasma of the twenty-first century. If Lot can make it, maybe we can too!

1. Ellen G. White, *Patriarchs and Prophets* (Mountain View, Calif.: Pacific Press®, 1958), 127; emphasis added.

2. Ibid., 156.

3. Ibid., 135.

4. "Commentary on Genesis 13," in 1599 Geneva Study Bible, note i.

5. Melancthon W. Jacobus, *Notes, Critical and Explanatory, on the Book of Genesis: From the Creation to the Covenant* (New York: Robert Carter & Brothers, 1865), 243.

6. Matthew Henry, "Genesis XIII," in *Genesis to Deuteronomy*, vol. 1 of *Commentary on the Whole Bible* (Grand Rapids, Mich.: Christian Classics Ethereal Library, 2000), 92, http://www.ccel.org/ccel/henry/mhc1.Gen.xiv.html; emphasis in original.

7. White, *Patriarchs and Prophets*, 169.

8. Ibid., 160.

9. Ibid., 141.

10. Ibid., 161.

11. Ibid., 167, 168; emphasis added.

12. Ibid., 139.

Questions for Reflection and Discussion

1. Scripture says that by beholding we become changed (2 Corinthians 3:18). How might this apply to Lot's living in Sodom? To his family? To us?

2. Did Sodom and Gomorrah cross some kind of boundary line? What do you think that line was? How can we become aware of such boundary lines? How can we avoid getting too close to the edge?

3. What kind of example do you think Lot provided for his family? What are a father's responsibilities as an example? A mother's responsibilities?

4. How could Peter call Lot righteous despite his drunkenness and the incest with his daughters? How much responsibility for those incidents belonged to Lot and how much to his daughters?

5. What effect might Lot's witness as a believer have had on the inhabitants of Sodom?

6. How much like Sodom and Gomorrah is our world today? Should we withdraw from it entirely? How should we relate to it?

7. Do you think Lot's wife was lost or just punished temporally (in this life) and not eternally?

Chapter 3
Ishmael, a Son of Promise?

Ishmael, a son of promise?

I can hear someone ask, "Aren't you getting him mixed up with Isaac?" And someone else saying, "Why is there even any question? All we have to do is look at Galatians 4:28, 29, 'Isn't it clear, friends, that you, *like Isaac*, are children of *promise*? In the days of Hagar and Sarah, the child who came from faithless connivance (Ishmael) harassed the child who came—empowered by the Spirit—from the faithful promise (Isaac)' " (*The Message*; emphasis added).

On the question of Ishmael being a son of promise, Galatians 4:30, 31 does seem to put the nail in the coffin: "Isn't it clear that the harassment you are now experiencing from the Jerusalem heretics follows that old pattern? There is a Scripture that tells us what to do. 'Expel the slave mother with her son, for the slave son will not inherit with the free son.' Isn't that conclusive? We are not children of the slave woman, but of the free woman" (*The Message*).

Very clear indeed. Isaac, not Ishmael, is the son of promise.

But wait! Might there be an intriguing shade of difference between *"the* son of promise" and *"a* son of promise"? Let's think on.

There are remarkable similarities between Ishmael and Isaac, as well there should be. They both had the same father: Abraham. They were both born in Abraham's old age—Abraham was eighty-six when Ishmael was born and one hundred at the birth of Isaac, which, of course means Ishmael was the firstborn son of Abraham. They were both sons of promise; God promised both of them multitudinous descendants—Ishmael as well as Isaac (see Genesis 16:10). So the blessings promised both sons were very similar. They were both named by God Himself, even before they were born. In fact, Ishmael was the very first one in sacred Scripture whom God named before his birth.

And you could hardly argue about Ishmael's pedigree. He was indeed a chip off the old Abrahamic block, so there really isn't any question about "genes" in his case. It would seem at first glance that Ishmael and Isaac started off on a level playing field. Opportunities, privileges, potential, promises, blessings? Pretty much equal.

However, there is one very significant detail in Scripture that makes the separation between Ishmael and Isaac as wide as the mouth of the Amazon River. There's a triad of names that the Bible mentions at least seventeen times: "Abraham, Isaac, and Jacob." These names are always mentioned as God's gold standard of character, faithfulness, and favor. And never once is the trio "Abraham, Ishmael, and Nebajoth (Ishmael's firstborn son)." There are reasons aplenty, but let's look first at some of the history surrounding Ishmael and then give credit where credit is due and examine some interesting and beautiful positives in his life story.

The firstborn son

Ishmael was indeed Abraham's firstborn son. When Abraham was eighty-five years old, he had no children *except by promise*. Then Ishmael was born. Never mind that his mother was an Egyptian maidservant of Sarah's named Hagar who, because of Sarah's insistence, became Abraham's other wife and Sarah's surrogate. In Ishmael, Abraham had the son he wanted, and he looked at Ishmael not only with eyes of love and pride, but also with eyes of faith, thinking that *he* would be the son of promise.

However, Genesis 17 pictures God regaling Abraham with a name change (from *Abram*, "the father is exalted," to *Abraham*, very likely meaning "father of a multitude"), the description of an everlasting covenant, and marvelous promises—all tied to a son that he *and Sarah* would have. But in his humanity and with a father's heart, Abraham cries out, "Oh, that Ishmael might live before You" (verse 18). In other words, this father's heart-cry was, "Please, Lord, please let Ishmael be the one—the son of promise." It was so hard for him to turn his love and thoughts and hopes from a son that he did have to a son that he didn't have and didn't see how he could have.

Genesis 16 reveals the trouble that had begun.

Sarai, Abram's wife, had no children. So Sarai took her servant, an Egyptian woman named Hagar, and gave her to Abram so she could bear his children. "The LORD has kept me from having any children," Sarai said to Abram. "Go and sleep with my servant. Perhaps I can have children through her." And Abram agreed. [Does it seem that Abraham struggled at all with compliance to Sarai's demand?] So Sarai, Abram's wife, took Hagar the Egyptian servant and gave her to Abram as a wife. (This happened ten years after Abram first arrived in the land of Canaan.) So Abram slept with Hagar, and she became pregnant. When Hagar knew she was pregnant, she began to treat her mistress Sarai with contempt. Then Sarai said to Abram, "It's all your fault! Now this servant of mine is pregnant, and she despises me, though I myself gave her the privilege of sleeping with you. The LORD will make you pay for doing this to me!" (Genesis 16:1–5, NLT).

Hadn't that been the whole idea—Sarai's whole idea—in the first place? Hadn't her plan been for Hagar to bear a son for Abram? Anyway, with Abram's permission to "deal with her as you see fit" (verse 6, NLT), Sarai took her revenge on Hagar for the taunting and made Hagar so miserable that she ran away. I don't know what the relationship between Sarai and her maid had been like before this, but now it blossomed into contention, dissension, distrust, and sharpened claws of jealousy, vindictiveness, and retaliation. And poor Ishmael didn't even know what was going on. He wasn't aware yet of his not-so-great start. He was born into a setting of lack of faith, of sin, of people following their own will and way, and deliberately setting aside God's will, instructions, and promises. What a climate of mistrust in which to grow up!

The son of promise

Now fast-forward approximately fourteen years. Isaac is born, and he isn't *a* son of promise but *the* son of promise. He's the son of Abraham *and* Sarah—you know, the man who was one hundred years old and the woman who was ninety. (Don't laugh!) He's the miracle child. He's God's idea. His birth is what God had promised in the first place. He's a faith child, not a lack-of-faith child.

Genesis 21:8 picks up the story: "So the child grew and was weaned. And Abraham made a great feast on the same day that Isaac was weaned." Eastern customs dictated that mothers nurse their children for three years, and the weaning of a child was then celebrated by a ritual feast. This feast "marks the close of infancy."[1] But evidently it also marked the beginning of Ishmael's open hostility toward his much younger half brother. Genesis 21:9 says, "Sarah saw the son of Hagar the Egyptian, whom she had borne to Abraham, *scoffing*"—as in sneering at, caring nothing for, looking down upon. Was the stage set this early for the hatred between Arabs, Ishmael's descendants, and Jews, Isaac's, that seems to be in full flower now? It would appear so.

Then came the final break. As the New Living Translation puts it, Sarah "turned to Abraham and demanded, 'Get rid of that servant and her son. He is not going to share the family inheritance with my son, Isaac. I won't have it!' " (Genesis 21:10).

Much to Abraham's distress and hurt, he found that Sarah and God were on the same side on this one. Genesis 21:12, 13 says, "God told Abraham, 'Do not be upset over the boy and your servant wife. Do just as Sarah says, for Isaac is the son through whom your descendants will be counted. But I will make a nation of the descendants of Hagar's son because he also is your son' " (NLT).

The negatives for Ishmael continue. Shall I list them?

- To begin with, God Himself painted a negative picture of Ishmael when he was yet unborn. *The Message* translation of Genesis 16:12 gives a very colorful, modern flavor to the prophecy about Ishmael: "He'll be a bucking bronco of a man, a real fighter, fighting and being fought, always stirring up trouble, always at odds with his family."

- Genesis 16:4 tells us that when Hagar became pregnant, she despised Sarah. Then "Sarai dealt harshly with her," and Hagar "fled from her presence" (verse 6).

- When Isaac was born, the whole encampment rejoiced for Abraham and Sarah. "But to Hagar this event was the overthrow of her fondly cherished ambitions. Ishmael, now a youth, had been regarded by all in the encampment as the heir of Abraham's wealth and the inheritor of the blessings promised to his descendants.

Now he was suddenly set aside; and in their disappointment, mother and son hated the child of Sarah."[2]

- The dissension this caused led to Hagar's second departure from the encampment—this time at Abraham's command (see Genesis 21:14).
- Beyond the fact that Ishmael lived in isolation in the wilderness and became a hunter, Genesis 21:21 tells us that "his mother took a wife for him from the land of Egypt." Hagar was Egyptian, so this isn't surprising. The negative element surfaces when we consider what kind of wife she was, and what kind of religion she had. Was she a God worshiper? Not likely.

Ellen White suggests, "Abraham's early teachings had not been without effect upon Ishmael, but the influence *of his wives* resulted in establishing idolatry in his family. Separated from his father, and embittered by the strife and contention of a home destitute of the love and fear of God, Ishmael was driven to choose the wild, marauding life of the desert chief."[3]

Not entirely bad

On the other hand, there were some laudable positives in Ishmael's beginnings that we should keep in mind. One of the very first positives is, as I mentioned earlier, that God Himself named Ishmael, calling him, literally, "God hears." This is no small thing. Was God interested in this wild man and his mother? Was he on God's mind? Did the God of the universe indeed concern Himself with an Egyptian maid and her as yet unborn child?

Remember, this was the first time that Hagar was separated from Abraham's household. And leaving was her choice, because "Sarai dealt harshly with her." She, then, in a mixture of anger, helplessness, and self-pity, left the only security she knew and headed into the wilderness. There she had the most unique experience of her life. "Now the Angel of the LORD found her by a spring of water in the wilderness" (Genesis 16:7). We don't know for sure whether this was actually an angel or the Lord Himself, but we do know that Hagar and her child were the special objects of God's love and care.

One commentator said beautifully, "The poor slave, the stranger, the Egyptian, suffering under the severity of her hasty, unbelieving mistress, is seen by the all-wise and merciful God. He permits her to go into the desert, provides the spring to quench her thirst, and sends the Angel of the covenant to instruct and comfort her. How gracious is God! . . . God delights to do his creatures good."[4]

We also know for sure that Hagar thought she had seen God Himself in this incident for she named the well *Beer Lahai Roi,* or "Well of the One Who Lives and Sees Me." So ever afterwards, she would be reminded of God's promise to her because whenever she mentioned Ishmael's name, she was saying, "God hears." When she called Ishmael for supper, she said, "God Hears, it's time for supper," and her thoughts would immediately turn to that amazing encounter with the Angel in the wilderness.

And there were more positives. The Angel of the Lord told her to return to her mistress Sarai and submit herself to her, but almost in the same breath, this "Angel" said to her, "I will multiply your descendants exceedingly, so that they shall not be counted for multitude" (Genesis 16:10). (Would an angel say that, or was it God Himself speaking?) Isn't there a striking parallel to the promise made to Abraham concerning Isaac and his descendants? (See Genesis 13:16.) So then Ishmael also was *a* son of promise.

When Abraham pleaded with God, "Oh, that Ishmael might live before You!" God said to him, "I have heard you. Behold, I have blessed him, and will make him fruitful, and will multiply him exceedingly. He shall beget twelve princes, and I will make him a great nation" (Genesis 17:18, 20).

The Seventh-day Adventist Bible Commentary tells us that "for generations Arabs refreshing themselves at this well were reminded that God here revealed Himself to their ancestor."[5] And the promise He made there to Hagar and later to Abraham regarding Ishmael has been strikingly fulfilled. Today, the Arab world reaches from the Arabian Sea to the Atlantic Ocean and from the Mediterranean Sea to sub-Saharan Africa. It comprises twenty-two countries and some 350 million people.

It seems that Genesis 25:9 is also a positive in the life of Ishmael. It tells us that when Abraham died, "his sons Isaac and Ishmael buried him in the cave of Machpelah." Funerals sometimes bring together loved ones who may not only have been separated but also estranged. We don't really know much about what Isaac and Ishmael's relationship was in the seventy-five years between Isaac's birth and Abraham's death. How much contact did they have? What were their feelings toward each other during those years?

We can only speculate. But at least the sons were together at the death of their father, and this was a good thing.

Ishmael's salvation

So, is Ishmael a candidate for the kingdom? On what basis might we have hope for his reunion in heaven with his father Abraham and his brother Isaac? Was death the end of the line for Isaac's contentious half brother? The Bible speaks about the saved sitting down with Abraham, *Isaac,* and Jacob in the kingdom (see Matthew 8:11). It doesn't mention anything about Ishmael. What about this poor, outsider half brother? Doesn't he get a crumb? Or will he end up like the rich man in Jesus' parable, asking his father Abraham to send Isaac with a drop of water to cool his tongue while he's roasting in the flames? Maybe he wasn't *the* son of promise, but doesn't being *a* son of promise count for anything?

Ishmael isn't on the roster of the faithful in Hebrews 11. The last time he is mentioned in the Old Testament is in 1 Chronicles 1:29–31, but it's only in a genealogy, with a list of his sons. And he isn't mentioned in the New Testament—not even once. But let me remind you of something. I believe it's an inspired something. Ellen White wrote, "In his [Ishmael's] latter days he repented of his evil ways and returned to his father's God."[6]

Isn't it a pretty thin hope? Are we looking at a "barely made it" scenario like that described in Jude, which calls believers to save some people "with fear, pulling them out of the fire" (verse 23)? Or is God interested in foxhole conversions, or last-minute, take-the-fire-escape conversions?

I think the answer to that last question is Yes! If the saved one is sincere, yes. If the saved one is genuinely repentant, yes. Of course, only God can read the heart, but we must remember that God isn't trying to keep as many people as possible out of heaven but to get as many people as possible in.

If God's goal were to save as few people as possible, He could easily reach it. There are a million reasons why none of us should be there. But Psalm 103:10 says, "He does not treat us as our sins deserve or repay us according to our iniquities" (NIV). And furthermore, Paul tells us in 1 Timothy 2:4 that God desires all people to be saved, and if justice so permitted, His amazing grace would be more than sufficient.

Does the last-minute believer really make it? Is the eleventh-hour servant going to get the same wages as those of us who have worked and sweated the whole day?

Christ Himself answered this question. You see, there was this thief on a cross next to Jesus. He was sinking for the last time into an ocean of lostness when he called to the precious Lifeguard to save him. And immediately, the Lifeguard threw him a life preserver.

A doctor friend of mine had been studying the Bible with a woman and appealing to her to accept Jesus Christ as her personal Savior—all to no avail. And then she was dying. Mostly comatose. In a last effort, this doctor leaned over and whispered close to her ear, "Would you like to ask Jesus to come into your heart right now and forgive you and save you?" She hadn't been responsive for some time, but she unmistakably nodded her head Yes. That's what she chose to do. Eleventh hour? Foxhole? Whatever! God will take anything He can get.

Ellen White says of Ishmael, "In his latter days he repented of his evil ways and returned to his father's God." Let's hear it for Ishmael! A son of promise. And God has the same salvation plan for any of Ishmael's descendants—Arabs and Muslims—who, like him, turn to the God of their father Abraham.

Forget that Ishmael was Abraham's lack-of-faith son. Forget Ishmael's wild, marauding lifestyle. Forget his late repentance. If we have faith, we'll sit down with Abraham and Isaac and Jacob—and Ishmael—in the kingdom of God.

---

1. *The Seventh-day Adventist Bible Commentary,* 1:344.

2. White, *Patriarchs and Prophets,* 146.

3. Ibid., 174; emphasis added.

4. Adam Clarke, *Clarke's Commentary,* vol. 1, *Genesis to Deuteronomy* (New York: Methodist Book Concern, n.d.), 112.

5. *The Seventh-day Adventist Bible Commentary,* 1:319.

6. White, *Patriarchs and Prophets,* 174.

Questions for Reflection and Discussion

1. Were Ishmael and his mother treated fairly? Explain your answer.

2. When two women such as Sarah and Hagar are at such odds with each other, can they both be in the kingdom? How?

3. Was Abraham's image as "father of the faithful" tarnished when he listened to Sarah and took Hagar as his wife?

4. How can people be blessed after they've made faithless moves outside of God's will?

5. Compare Isaac's life with Ishmael's. Do your sympathies lean towards one or the other? Are there lessons for your life?

6. How is our picture of God's character enhanced by His treatment of Ishmael—or is it marred?

7. Does Ishmael inspire you in any way?

Chapter 4
Band of Brothers

The brothers all had the same father but four different mothers. Jacob was the father. Leah, Rachel, Bilhah, and Zilpah were the mothers. The brothers, at least the first eleven, were born into a toxic mix of envy, jealousy, rivalry, and contention.

In order to understand this band of brothers better, you have to know the climate they each experienced. It may be best pictured in Genesis 29 and 30 in *The Message* paraphrase, beginning with chapter 29, verse 31.

When GOD realized that Leah was unloved [Jacob "loved Rachel more than Leah," verse 30], he opened her womb. But Rachel was barren. Leah became pregnant and had a son. She named him Reuben (Look-It's-a-Boy!). "This is a sign," she said, "that GOD has seen my misery; and a sign that now my husband will love me."

She became pregnant again and had another son. "GOD heard," she said, "that I was unloved and so he gave me this son also." She named this one Simeon (GOD-Heard). She became pregnant yet again—another son. She said, "Now maybe my husband will connect with me—I've given him three sons!" That's why she named him Levi (Connect). She became pregnant a final time and had a fourth son. She said, "This time I'll praise GOD." So she named him Judah (Praise-GOD). Then she stopped having children.

When Rachel realized that she wasn't having any children for Jacob, she became jealous of her sister [Leah]. She told Jacob, "Give me sons or I'll die!"

Jacob got angry with Rachel and said, "Am I God? Am I the one who refused you babies?"

Rachel said, "Here's my maid Bilhah. Sleep with her. Let her substitute for me so I can have a child through her and build a family." So she gave him her maid Bilhah for a wife and Jacob slept with her. Bilhah became pregnant and gave Jacob a son.

Rachel said, "God took my side and vindicated me. He listened to me and gave me a son." She named him Dan (Vindication). Rachel's maid Bilhah became pregnant again and gave Jacob a second son. Rachel said, "I've been in an all-out fight with my sister—and I've won." So she named him Naphtali (Fight).

When Leah saw that she wasn't having any more children, she gave her maid Zilpah to Jacob for a wife. Zilpah had a son for Jacob. Leah said, "How fortunate!" and she named him Gad (Lucky). When Leah's maid Zilpah had a second son for Jacob, Leah said, "A happy day! The women will congratulate me in my happiness." So she named him Asher (Happy).

One day during the wheat harvest Reuben found some mandrakes* in the field and brought them home to his mother Leah. Rachel asked Leah, "Could I please have some of your son's mandrakes?"

Leah said, "Wasn't it enough that you got my husband away from me? And now you also want my son's mandrakes?"

Rachel said, "All right. I'll let him sleep with you tonight in exchange for your son's love-apples."

When Jacob came home that evening from the fields, Leah was there to meet him: "Sleep with me tonight; I've bartered my son's mandrakes for a night with you." So he slept with her that night. God listened to Leah; she became pregnant and gave Jacob a fifth son. She said, "God rewarded me for giving my maid to my husband." She named him Issachar (Bartered). Leah became pregnant yet again and gave Jacob a sixth son, saying, "God has given me a great gift. This time my husband will honor me with gifts— I've given him six sons!" She named him Zebulun (Honor). Last of all she had a daughter and named her Dinah.

And then God remembered Rachel. God listened to her and opened her womb. She became pregnant and had a son. She said,

---

*A plant that the ancients believed stimulated sensual desire and increased fertility.

"God has taken away my humiliation." She named him Joseph (Add), praying, "May GOD add yet another son to me."

That's the story of the beginning of the eleven. When Benjamin, number twelve, came along, his mother died giving birth to him (Genesis 35:17, 18). So envy, jealousy, rivalry, and contention marred the world into which the band of brothers was born. One father. Four mothers. The best way to track the brothers and their mothers is by reading the scorecard in Genesis 35: "The sons of Jacob were twelve: the sons of Leah were Reuben, Jacob's firstborn, and Simeon, Levi, Judah, Issachar, and Zebulun; the sons of Rachel were Joseph and Benjamin; the sons of Bilhah, Rachel's maidservant, were Dan and Naphtali; and the sons of Zilpah, Leah's maidservant, were Gad and Asher" (verses 22–26).

We well remember that Jacob's life was forever marred by the deceit that he and his mother practiced on Isaac. Jacob pretended to be his brother Esau, and by an outright lying deception, he obtained the coveted spiritual and financial birthright that should have gone to Esau. Soon after, he was fleeing from home for fear of his brother's vengeance. This flagrant departure from God's will was to haunt Jacob for many years—in fact, until he spent the night at the brook Jabbok, wrestling with Christ. The night on which he was humbled, broken, and made repentant and on which the Lord gave him a new name: *Israel,* "Contender With God." That long.

Unfortunately, parents can pass on their proclivities, their tendencies, to their children.

Like father, like sons

The picture of Jacob, the "heel grabber," portrayed in Genesis 27 isn't pretty. Oh, we know that the plot started with Rebekah. She laid the mother-son relationship on Jacob and commanded him to play the role she assigned him in the plot. But how can you help but think that, very likely, Jacob was fantasizing about all the blessings and benefits, honor and status that would accrue to him if it all worked out. At any rate, he was totally complicit.

So, deceit was in the genes of all the sons of Jacob. It came from their father, from their grandmother Rebekah, from their great-grandfather Abraham, and—we might as well admit it—from Adam and Eve. The sins of the fathers! The seeds were sown, and, as we shall see, they sprouted and bore fruit in the sons. Wasn't this reflected in the words of the second commandment: "Visiting the iniquity of the fathers upon the children to the third and fourth generations" (Exodus 20:5)? That's the way it is on this sin-infected planet. The book *Patriarchs and Prophets* puts it like this: "As these sons arrived at manhood they developed serious faults. The results of polygamy were manifest in the household. This terrible evil tends to dry up the very springs of love, and its influence weakens the most sacred ties. The jealousy of the several mothers had embittered the family relation, the children had grown up contentious and impatient of control, and the father's life was darkened with anxiety and grief."[1]

Nothing much is said of the growing-up years of these brothers. Their characters came on display later, especially in the incident that involved their sister Dinah. The sad story is told graphically in Genesis 34. A young member of the local royalty, Shechem, was smitten with Dinah's beauty, and he forced himself on her.

I don't know this for sure, but I can't help but wonder if this whole sad incident didn't begin with a decision Dinah made. "Dinah the daughter of Leah, whom she had borne to Jacob, *went out to see the daughters of the land*" (Genesis 34:1; emphasis added). *The Seventh-day Adventist Bible Commentary* makes this observation on her choice: "The Jewish historian Josephus mentions an old tradition to the effect that the Shechemites were engaged in festivities . . . , and that Dinah wanted to join the girls of Shechem in their round of pleasure. The language implies the paying of a friendly visit, possibly even that Dinah was in the habit of associating with the girls of Shechem."[2] The danger of this practice is pointed out in 1 Corinthians 15:33, "Don't let anyone deceive you. Associating with bad people will ruin decent people" (GOD'S WORD).

However, we aren't speaking about the band of daughters but about the band of brothers and their characteristics. Shechem's horrible violation of Dinah elicited from her brothers a display of deceit and violence that far overshadowed what their father Jacob had done.

Perhaps you remember the sordid story. Shechem asked his father, Hamor, to obtain from Jacob, Dinah's father, permission to marry her. Enter the band of brothers: "But the sons of Jacob answered Shechem and Hamor his father, and spoke deceitfully, because he had defiled Dinah their sister" (Genesis 34:13). They said that he could have her as his wife if all the males in the city were circumcised. Hamor and Shechem happily agreed to this, and the surgery was carried out. But three days later, while all the men "were in pain," Simeon and Levi, two of Dinah's full brothers, took their swords into the city and killed all of the hapless males (verse 25). The other brothers were complicit in this violence, as Genesis 34:27 says, "The sons of Jacob came upon the slain, and plundered the city, because their sister had been defiled." They took everything in sight, the men's animals, their crops plus all their little ones and their wives. Not exactly a fulfillment of the second great commandment, to "love your neighbor as yourself" (Mark 12:31). The story of Dinah is an example of the strong unlikelihood of the brothers making it into the kingdom of God, but it certainly wasn't the only example. Unfortunately, their unlikelihood continued, for Genesis 35:22 says, "It happened, when Israel dwelt in that land, that Reuben went and lay with Bilhah his father's concubine; and Israel [Jacob] heard about it."

Reuben was Jacob's firstborn. His was the birthright privilege. His was the special inheritance. At least that's what should have been. But this grievous sin at Eder made Reuben unworthy of the birthright blessings. For a few moments of lustful, unlawful pleasure, he threw it all overboard. Does this not remind you of his uncle Esau and the bowl of lentils?

I find it distasteful to highlight the sins of others and their flagrant departures from God's law and God's will, but it must be done. We must do it because the Bible doesn't gloss over the sins of the people of God, so neither should we. We must point out the humanity of God's people of the past and their subsequent changes and victories. We must do this so we won't despair over our own missteps and mistakes and believe that our own unlikelihood ensures that we have but a slim-to-none chance of making it into the kingdom.

The highlighting continues. Now we must recount the hatred the band of brothers felt towards Joseph. It wasn't enough that Joseph was a tattletale kid brother, who reported to his father some of the bad things the brothers were doing (see Genesis 37:2). Tattling doesn't exactly encourage warm fuzzies on the part of those whose tales are being told, but there was more. Scripture says it outright: "Israel loved Joseph more than all his children, because he was the son of his old age" (verse 3). And the brothers sensed it—knew it.

Then Jacob put the flaming match to the gasoline. He made Joseph a coat of "many colors," an elaborately embroidered coat, and the brothers' jealousy exploded (verse 3). "When his brothers saw that their father loved him more than all his brothers, they hated him and could not speak peaceably to him" (verse 4). This wasn't just passing disgust or mild dislike. It was a raw, jealous hatred that burned hotter and hotter.

Could it get worse? Yes. Because Joseph had two dreams. In the first, he and his brothers were binding sheaves in the field, and his sheaf stood up and their sheaves bowed down to his. Even Jacob reprimanded Joseph about the second dream. In it the sun, the moon, and eleven stars—representing his father, mother, and brothers—bowed down to him. This made the brothers add envy to their hatred.

So, the stage was set for that fateful encounter when Joseph found his brothers in Dothan. Scripture says, "They spotted him off in the distance. By the time he got to them they had cooked up a plot to kill him" (Genesis 37:18–20, *The Message*). The old parental DNA had played itself out in this formula: Jealousy + Envy + Hatred = Murder. Given the chance, that formula works every time—and now the brothers had the chance.

Through the intervention of Reuben, the brothers decided to reduce the evil by one step, so they sold their brother Joseph to the Ishmaelites and dipped his precious coat in blood, leaving their father to conclude that an animal had killed Joseph. Perfectly perfidious! First John 2:11 says, "He who hates his brother is in darkness . . . and does not know where he is going, because the darkness has blinded his eyes." Of course, in the days of the band of brothers, these words hadn't been written yet, but their consciences knew the truth of them anyway.

To complete the picture of the unlikelihood of the band of brothers making it into the kingdom, we could add to their record the incestuous harlotry of Judah with his daughter-in-law. And we could recount Jacob's prophecy, recorded in Genesis 49, regarding each of his sons. For the most part, because of the sinful characteristics that prophecy delineated, it was more like cursings than blessings. Ellen White summed up the record in these words:

> Jacob had sinned, and had deeply suffered. Many years of toil, care, and sorrow had been his since the day when his great sin caused him to flee from his father's tents. A homeless fugitive, separated from his mother, whom he never saw again; laboring seven years for her whom he loved, only to be basely cheated; toiling twenty years in the service of a covetous and grasping kinsman; seeing his wealth increasing, and sons rising around him, but

finding little joy in the contentious and divided household; distressed by his daughter's shame, by her brothers' revenge, by the death of Rachel, by the unnatural crime of Reuben, by Judah's sin, by the cruel deception and malice practiced toward Joseph—how long and dark is the catalogue of evils spread out to view! Again and again he had reaped the fruit of that first wrong deed. *Over and over he saw repeated among his sons the sins of which he himself had been guilty.*[3]

Something had to happen. For those who had hated to the point of murder to become likely prospects for citizenship in the kingdom of heaven, rather than in the kingdom of eternal darkness, something had to change.

From unlikely to likely

Scripture draws a veil of silence over the next years of the band of unlikely brothers. From Genesis 39 to 41, nothing good is recorded, but neither is anything bad. Just nothing at all. Instead, the whole focus is on Joseph, Jacob's embroidered-coat-of-many-colors pet. That period was about thirteen years long, for Joseph was seventeen when he was sold into Egypt and thirty when he became the second in command in that country. No mention is made of the brothers until the pharaoh set Joseph "over all the land of Egypt" (Genesis 41:45). Not until a "famine was over all the face of the earth" (verse 56). Not until Genesis 42 do the brothers reappear and cross paths again with the brother whom they had so despised and hated.

Consequently, there's no record of how the brothers' hearts and minds and lives might have changed during those silent years. We don't know if their sin was ever before them. We don't know if they were often haunted by memories of the upturned, pleading face of their brother as he was taken off into slavery in Egypt. We don't know for sure if they truly sorrowed for what they had done or truly repented, or whether or not they made things right with God regarding their previous life. *But something happened during those years!* Genesis 42–45 tells us about the amazing changes that had taken place in the lives of the brothers.

- Their humility (Genesis 42:6)
- Their deference to authority (Genesis 42:10)

- Their honesty (Genesis 42:11–13)
- Their acknowledgment of their guilt (Genesis 42:21)
- Their sensitive, responsive hearts (Genesis 42:28, 35)
- Their assumption of responsibility for their actions (Genesis 42:37)
- Their transparency (Genesis 43:7)
- Their brokenness (Genesis 44:16)
- Their remorse (Genesis 44:18–34)
- Their desire to be forgiven (Genesis 50)

People can change. Hearts can soften. New directions can be taken. Miracles of grace can happen. The most unlikely candidates for the kingdom can become rightful candidates through Jesus Christ and His patience, His love, His long-suffering, His matchless grace. This is why we must always look upon others with eyes open to what they can become. As long as life lasts, people have the potential of becoming what God wants them to become through His blessed Son.

I love the proofs of the brothers' change that Ellen White recorded, "During the years since Joseph had been separated from his brothers, these sons of Jacob had changed in character. Envious, turbulent, deceptive, cruel, and revengeful they had been; but now, when tested by adversity [tests that Joseph had arranged], they were shown to be unselfish, true to one another, devoted to their father, and, themselves middle-aged men, [still] subject to his authority."[4]

After Joseph had administered one of his tests and had seen and heard Judah's deep distress, he "was satisfied. He had seen in his brothers the fruits of true repentance."[5] So he had graciously revealed himself to them and, instead of blaming them for their hateful, treacherous act towards him, had said, "*God* sent me before you to preserve a posterity for you in the earth" (Genesis 45:7; emphasis added) and had kissed them and wept over them. Then "they humbly confessed their sin and entreated his forgiveness. They had long suffered anxiety and remorse, and now they rejoiced that he was still alive."[6]

Beyond this, "another act of humiliation remained for the ten brothers. They now confessed to their father the deceit and cruelty that for so many years had embittered his life and theirs. Jacob had not suspected them of so base a sin, but he saw that all had been overruled for good, and he forgave and blessed his erring children."[7]

While, except for Joseph, the names of the band of brothers aren't mentioned in Hebrews 11, we mustn't forget that John the revelator, under inspiration, records their names in connection with the redeemed at the coming of Christ. The sealed ones—the special ones—the one hundred and forty-four thousand. (See Revelation 7:4–8. See also Revelation 21:12.) That's quite an honor for the band of brothers, considering their unlikely past!

---

1. White, *Patriarchs and Prophets,* 208, 209.

2. *The Seventh-day Adventist Bible Commentary,* 1:412.

3. White, *Patriarchs and Prophets,* 237, 238; emphasis added.

4. Ibid., 225.

5. Ibid., 230.

6. Ibid., 231.

7. Ibid., 232.

Questions for Reflection and Discussion

1. Do you see the band of brothers as "real men" and Joseph as a "goody, goody two-shoes"? Explain.

2. What words best describe your feelings about the brothers? Disappointment? Hope? Inspiration?

3. If the brothers had all died in some kind of a flaming chariot crash just after they sold Joseph to the Ishmaelites, do you think there would have been any possibility of their being in the kingdom? Why or why not?

4. How much blame should parents be assessed for the actions of their children? How much blame should Jacob and his wives bear for the actions of their sons? How much blame should the brothers themselves bear?

5. Is it easier to compare yourself to weak, failing people like the band of brothers or to spiritual giants like Daniel and Paul? However you answer, why is this so?

6. What lessons does the band of brothers teach about judging people before their time?

7. What have you learned about the character of God from His dealings with the band of brothers?

Chapter 5
Rahab the Harlot

Our introduction to Rahab is very abrupt. The very first verse of chapter 2 of the book of Joshua mentions the two spies who went to Jericho to "view the land," and then says they "came to the house of a harlot named Rahab, and lodged there." Now, you have to wonder a little. How did they know about Rahab, her house, and being able to "lodge there"? Did she have that wide-ranging a reputation? Was she in the Yellow Pages? Did she live in a certain district, or was there a red light—or at least a red lamp— burning outside her home? Were there little signs on sticks along the road into Jericho that advertised her "business"? The Bible doesn't fill in a lot of the details, and we don't need to know a lot of the details, but one can't help but wonder a little.

Whatever the case, we meet Rahab right at the beginning of the book of Joshua. Ordinarily, when you're introducing a person to someone, you might well start out by mentioning some nice, positive things about that person. You wouldn't usually say, "I'd like you to meet a good friend of mine who's spent a lot of time in prison, is a hard-core alcoholic, and has committed adultery more times than you can count." But, unlike us, the Bible always tells it like it is. It doesn't conceal the warts, blemishes, foibles, failings, and stumblings. It puts them all out there. God is no respecter of persons, and the Bible doesn't gloss over well-seasoned reputations. We would do well to take a closer look at Rahab's name, her city, her environment, her times, and her profession so that we can better understand this unlikely candidate for the kingdom.

Rahab's early life and times

Today, we most often choose names for our children simply because

of the way they sound. Seldom do we pay much attention to the meaning of the name. But in ancient times, names and their meanings carried
more significance. *Rahab* can mean "roomy, . . . broad, large, at liberty,
proud, wide."[1] Origen, an early church leader, theologian, and philoso-
pher, sees in this name a type of the church of Christ, which extends
throughout the world and receives sinners.[2] That's an interesting observation, particularly when you remember that Rahab was in the lineage
of Christ.

So, Rahab's name is just fine. It's too bad that the epithet *the harlot* is at-
tached to it so often. How would you like to have that tag after your name
on your résumé and passport and in your church membership directory?
But from the time of Joshua, around 1405 B.C., and on—in other words, for
the past thirty-five hundred years—this woman has been known as "Rahab
the harlot."

Some Bible scholars and expositors seem to have had a difficult time
dealing with Rahab's rather colorful renown. Apparently, they believe that
it casts a shadow on Christ. So, in his commentary on Joshua, for instance,
Adam Clarke writes, "I am fully satisfied that the term . . . *zonah* in the text,
which we translate *harlot,* should be rendered *tavern* or *innkeeper,* or *host-
ess.*"[3] Some Jewish writers and other Protestant commentators have made
the same argument.

There is indeed a measure of linguistic evidence that points toward that
meaning. But then, was David a pure, spotless progenitor of Christ? And
was it necessary that each person in the lineage of Christ be absolutely spotless in character? Is it not rather fascinating that in Matthew's recounting of
Christ's ancestors he mentions only three women, in addition to Mary, by
name: Tamar, who was guilty of incest; Ruth, who as a Moabitess was an
outsider; and Rahab the harlot?

James Strong, in his *Exhaustive Concordance,* suggests a very different picture than did Adam Clarke—as do many other scholars and commentators.
His definition of the verb based on the same root as the word translated
harlot uses these phrases: "to commit adultery . . . (cause to) commit forni-
cation, . . . (be an, play the) harlot, (cause to be, play the) whore, (commit,
fall to) whoredom, (cause to) go a-whoring, whorish."[4] And doesn't that
profession make sense in the story? Wouldn't it have been less conspicuous
for the spies to slip into a harlot's house rather than for them to spend the
night in a fourteenth-century B.C. Motel 6?

The New Testament confirms this unflattering interpretation. It uses the expression *Rahab the harlot* twice—and there's no ambiguity about the meaning of the Greek word it uses—*pŏrnē.*[5] This word means "harlot" or "whore." That word is the root of our English words *pornography* and *pornographic* and so on. Five of the seven times Rahab is mentioned in God's Word she is called a harlot—what we today call a prostitute. We ought not to belabor the matter. Let's face it; Rahab was a loose woman who plied her trade in the oldest profession known.*

Rahab's environment

One might say that Rahab came by her epithet naturally, but she came by it geographically and societally as well. Jericho wasn't exactly the place where God worshipers would go for a weekend spiritual retreat. The name of the city may mean "city of the moon (god)." Ellen White notes that "Jericho was one of the principal seats of idol worship, being especially devoted to Ashtaroth, the goddess of the moon. Here centered all that was vilest and most degrading in the religion of the Canaanites."[6] And *The Seventh-day Adventist Bible Commentary* says, "The peoples on the eastern seaboard of the Mediterranean were as corrupt and depraved as any who have ever dwelt on this earth. They made a religion of lust."[7]

The debauchery of these pagans has to be the reason for the severe instructions God Himself gave concerning their destruction as the Israelites conquered Palestine. Deuteronomy 7:2 says, "When the LORD your God delivers them over to you, you shall conquer them and *utterly destroy them*" (emphasis added). This meant the men and the women, the young and the old, the infants and the animals—every living thing. "You shall make no covenant with them *nor show mercy* to them" (verse 2; emphasis added). In *The Message,* Eugene Peterson translates Deuteronomy 7:5 this way:

Here's what you are to do:

Tear apart their altars stone by stone,

---

*We don't know whether Rahab was a temple prostitute or whether she had her own business.

smash their phallic pillars,
chop down their sex-and-religion Asherah groves,
set fire to their carved god-images.

So, the record in Joshua 6:21 states that when Joshua took Jericho, "They utterly destroyed all that was in the city, both man and woman, young and old, ox and sheep and donkey, with the edge of the sword." There had to be antediluvian-like corruption in Jericho and its environs for the Lord to pronounce such a terrible sentence on every living thing.

Since Rahab came out of this societal cesspool, it isn't really surprising to find her telling lies when she was asked about the two Israelite men who came to her house. Here's the way the Bible tells it in Joshua 2:2–6.

It was told the king of Jericho, saying, "Behold, men have come here tonight from the children of Israel to search out the country." So the king of Jericho sent to Rahab, saying, "Bring out the men who have come to you, who have entered your house, for they have come to search out all the country." Then the woman took the two men and hid them. So she said, "Yes, the men came to me [the truth, so far], but I did not know where they were from. And it happened as the gate was being shut, when it was dark, that the men went out. Where the men went I do not know; pursue them quickly, for you may overtake them." (But she had brought them up to the roof and hidden them with the stalks of flax, which she had laid in order on the roof.)

So, Rahab told a series of lies in order to save the lives of the Israelite men. Joseph Fletcher, the father of situational ethics, would've had no problem with this at all. Nor would it be a problem for a very large percentage of our population, in whose psyche Fletcher's position has become the norm. *The Seventh-day Adventist Bible Commentary* has a cogent comment on Rahab's dilemma. "Rahab was faced with what seemed to her a choice between a greater and a lesser evil: to share in the responsibility of the death of two men whom she believed to be messengers of God, or to tell a lie and save them. To a Christian a lie can never be justified, but to a person like Rahab light comes but gradually."[8]

One might ask, "Is there a big difference between breaking commandment number seven and commandment number nine?" And, of course, there really isn't. Sin is sin. According to James 2:10, break one commandment, and you break them all. We aren't really looking at degrees of sinfulness here, but rather at the spiritual condition of one woman from Jericho.

Altogether then, speaking as she spoke, living as she lived, living *where* she lived, she didn't have great prospects of being a kingdom candidate. But then Christ didn't come into the world to invite the pious, the righteous, the virtuous people, and the "insiders" into the kingdom, but rather the sick, the sinful, the degraded, and the lost ones.

Her change and her faith

It's a miracle that beautiful, fragrant lilies grow out of the muck of a foul, smelly swamp. What kind of a miracle is it when a woman like Rahab emerges from her background, her place, and her times and becomes a follower of God, clothed in the pure white raiment of the righteousness of Jesus Christ, her life exuding the fragrance of a God-centered life, and then she is placed in faith's Hall of Fame in Hebrews 11? What a story! What a change! What an exhibit of what God can do in the life of anyone who hears, believes, receives, and heeds the things of God!

How did this happen? God hasn't revealed most of the details, but some of them are evident and intriguing. Rahab told the Israelite spies what she knew of them and of their God. Her comments give telling insights into the change and how it might have come about.

> "*I know that the* LORD *has given you the land,* that the terror of you has fallen on us, and that all the inhabitants of the land are fainthearted because of you. *For we have heard* how the LORD dried up the water of the Red Sea for you when you came out of Egypt, and what you did to the two kings of the Amorites who were on the other side of the Jordan, Sihon and Og, whom you utterly destroyed. And as soon as we heard these things, our hearts melted; neither did there remain any more courage in anyone because of you, *for the* LORD *your God, He is God in heaven above and on earth beneath*" (Joshua 2:9–11; emphasis added).

Doesn't it seem that the testimony of this heathen harlot back there in the fourteenth century B.C. is about as striking as the declaration made by the (somewhat) enlightened Peter, "You are the Christ, the Son of the living God" (Matthew 16:16)? Did someone send Rahab the *Signs of the Times®* from the Palestinian press? Did she live next door to a Seventh-day Israelite? Had someone arranged for her to take the correspondence course from the VOP (the Voice of the Prophets)? She certainly hadn't had enough time with the two spies to learn much about God from them. But she must have had some kind of exposure to God, and she did have it.

The main key to understanding the awakening of her conscience has to be the words in Joshua 2:10, "For we have heard . . ." Ellen White supports this. She says,

> The inhabitants of Canaan had been granted ample opportunity for repentance. Forty years before, the opening of the Red Sea and the judgments upon Egypt had testified to the supreme power of the God of Israel. And now the overthrow of the kings of Midian, of Gilead and Bashan, had further shown that Jehovah was above all gods. The holiness of His character and His abhorrence of impurity had been evinced in the judgments visited upon Israel for their participation in the abominable rites of Baalpeor. *All these events were known to the inhabitants of Jericho, and there were many who shared Rahab's conviction, though they refused to obey it, that Jehovah, the God of Israel, "is God in heaven above, and upon the earth beneath."*[9]

Add to this the fact that Jericho was on the route of the caravan trade carried on between Babylon and Egypt. Traders from these countries were passing through, and some of them who wanted a certain kind of place to stay overnight might well have heard about the "God happenings." Also, just a short time before, Israel had once again passed through the floodwaters of the Jordan, and a couple million people crossing the Jordan on the dry river bottom wasn't something that would be kept secret. So Rahab, along with virtually everyone else in the area, could easily have learned about God, His power, His supremacy, and His care for His people.

But beyond all this, we're seeing evidence of the infinite mercy of God for heathen idolaters who, to our eyes, appear to be enclosed in the midnight darkness of ignorance and superstition, blind to the light of God and the hope of salvation. We're seeing that they aren't shut away from God's notice, from His love and His care—simply because "God can travel where no teacher comes, and can enter where no truth is known, and can commend Himself to hearts that seem incapable of appreciating His charms. And so here, without guide, teacher, or companion, she [Rahab] rises to the light of God."[10]

Ellen White says succinctly, "The knowledge of Jehovah that had thus come to her, proved her salvation. . . . Her conversion was not an isolated case of God's mercy toward idolaters who acknowledged His divine authority."[11]

We don't know how much knowledge about God Rahab had, but then, nor do we know how much knowledge people must have to find salvation. But we do know that Rahab had faith. She confessed her faith in a striking manner when she said, "The LORD your God, He is God in heaven above and on earth beneath." Paul tells us that "God has dealt to *each one* a measure of faith" (Romans 12:3; emphasis added). It seems to me that however much faith is in that "measure," it's enough.

So, Rahab had enough faith and enough conviction to hide the two spies. Whatever else she might have been, she wasn't weak and afraid. She put her life on the line, risked it all, because the measure of faith she had moved her to carry out a dangerous, courageous course of action.

Rahab also had enough reasoned faith to think about and provide for her entire family: "Now therefore, I beg you, swear to me by the LORD, since I have shown you kindness, that you also will show kindness to my father's house, and give me a true token, and spare my father, my mother, my brothers, my sisters, and all that they have, and deliver our lives from death" (Joshua 2:12, 13).*

Rahab had faith enough to do exactly what the Israelite men asked her to do. They had told her to "bind this line of scarlet cord in the window through which you let us down" (verse 18). She did that. They also instructed her to "bring your father, your mother, your brothers, and all your father's household to your own home" (verse 18). She did that as well. Faith and works go hand in hand, and in that order: faith first, and second, works—acting on that faith, working out that faith, making that faith perfect. And

---

*It's interesting that she didn't mention a husband or children.

with that faith, people can go from being harlots—or from any other role in life—right into heaven itself.

Rahab's legacy

It is startling to remember that Rahab became the wife of Salmon; her child was Boaz and her daughter-in-law, Ruth the Moabitess; her great-grandson was David; and Jesus of Nazareth had her blood, her DNA, in His veins. Not a bad legacy for Red-light Rahab! And more than that even, Inspiration clearly establishes Rahab's position as born again, a child of God, "saved." Hebrews 11:31 says, "By faith the *harlot* Rahab [there it is again] did not perish with those who did not believe, when she had received the spies in peace" (emphasis added).

On January 16, 2007, a site on the Internet called Breitbart.com carried a story from the Netherlands. It announced that "Amsterdam's red light district is reportedly to receive a bronze statue dedicated to prostitutes around the world. . . . The statue would be a first of its kind and that it had received the blessing of the city authorities."[12]

There's a monument to Rahab, too, but it isn't the one to be erected in Amsterdam, but the one that the Holy Spirit erected in Hebrews 11:31. Do we realize what we see there? Rahab's in faith's Hall of Fame. She's in the same league as giants of faith like Enoch, Abraham, and Moses. She has been stamped with the "good heaven's keeping" seal of approval. She's become Righteous Rahab. Whatever the requirements for heaven might be—sinless perfection, or whatever—she met them *by faith!*

Heaven will be filled with the most unlikely people: prostitutes, child abusers, pornographers, drunkards, murderers, adulterers—and whatever *we* may have been in the past. But it will be filled with new, changed, converted, forgiven versions of these people—versions who reflect the image of Jesus fully.

One final note about Rahab. In heaven, she won't carry the stigma, the opprobrium, of the moniker she bore so many times: "Rahab the harlot." We know she won't because of what Jesus Himself says in Revelation 3:12, "He who overcomes, I will make him a pillar in the temple of My God, and he shall go out no more. I will write on him the name of My God and the name of the city of My God, the New Jerusalem, which comes down out of heaven from My God. *And I will write on him* [and Rahab too] *My new name"* (emphasis added). In the kingdom, we'll all have new names—and no one will be attaching tags descriptive of our former lives!

---

1. James Strong, *Strong's Exhaustive Concordance of the Bible* (Iowa Falls, Iowa: Word Bible Publishers, 1989), Hebrew entry 7342.

2. Origen, *Homilies on Joshua*, trans. Barbara J. Bruce, ed. Cynthia White (Washington, D.C.: Catholic University of America Press, 2002), 47.

3. Clarke, *Clarke's Commentary*, vol. 2, *Joshua to Esther* (New York: Methodist Book Concern, n.d.), 11.

4. Strong, *Strong's Exhaustive Concordance*, Hebrew entry 2181.

5. Ibid., Greek entry 4204.

6. White, *Patriarchs and Prophets*, 487.

7. *The Seventh-day Adventist Bible Commentary*, 2:200.

8. Ibid., 2:183.

9. White, *Patriarchs and Prophets*, 492; emphasis added.

10. R. Glover, "Homilies by Various Authors [on the Book of Joshua 2:4]," in *Deuteronomy, Joshua & Judges*, vol. 3 of *The Pulpit Commentary*, eds. H. D. M. Spence and Joseph S. Exell (Grand Rapids, Mich.: Eerdmans, 1950), 36 (see homily on Joshua 2:40).

11. White, *Prophets and Kings*, 369.

12. AFP, "Amsterdam to Get Statue to World's Prostitutes," *Breibart*, January 16, 2007, http://www.breitbart.com/article.php?id=070116173159.3yvt2yr3&show_article=1.

Questions for Reflection and Discussion

1. Rahab lied (Joshua 2:4, 5). Was this a white lie? Was it all right with God? Are we looking at situational ethics?

2. What does God think of prostitutes? What do you think of prostitutes? How should we relate to prostitutes? To prostitution?

3. How much do people have to know before God will deliver them and count them among His people?

4. Joshua 6:17 indicates that the basis of Rahab and her family being counted among the faithful was "because she hid the messengers that we sent." Was this a matter of great faith or little faith? How much faith is enough to assure one a place in the kingdom?

5. What significance do you find in deliverance and salvation having come to Rahab's entire household?

6. Rahab was mentioned in Hebrews 11, the "faith chapter," and Manasseh wasn't. Why?

7. What comfort do you find in the story of Rahab?

Chapter 6
Barak . . . Who?

If you asked ten Christians to identify the Bible character named Barak, how many do you think could answer correctly? And how many do you think would be able to elaborate on details about his life and work and his place in sacred history? Do you recognize the name, and do you remember anything about him?

This quite unfamiliar Bible figure is mentioned a total of thirteen times in the Old Testament, all thirteen are in chapters 4 and 5 of the book of Judges. Significantly, he is mentioned one time in the New Testament. Still more significantly, his name is found in one of the most coveted places not only in the New Testament but in the entire Bible.

Where?

In the eleventh chapter of Hebrews, that Hall of Fame of Scripture's "faith greats."

So, why is Barak mentioned in this rather exalted company? Was he an Abraham?

No.

Was he a Moses?

Hardly.

Was he at least some kind of faith hero?

It seems quite unlikely.

Have many people named their sons *Barak* because of his amazing faith accomplishments?

Not that I'm aware of.

Maybe his faith was of such a stellar quality that it gave him an inside track with the God of heaven?

You'll have to decide. But he *is* there, in Scripture, not just in the Old

Testament book of Judges, but also right there in that faith chapter (see Hebrews 11:32).

Because of Barak's relative obscurity, you may be tempted to underestimate him. Don't do that. He *did* lead an army. He *was* a commander. God *was* able to use him. His army *did* destroy the enemies of Israel and of God. He *did* win a significant victory, and the land *did* have rest for forty years after—not a small achievement!

A closer look

Barak is first mentioned in Judges 4:6. From this very first mention on, he's overshadowed by someone else. A woman named Deborah. She was a prophetess and a judge in Israel. Let's get the setting.

"When Ehud was dead, the children of Israel *again did evil* in the sight of the LORD" (Judges 4:1; emphasis added). How many times was this recorded of the people of the Lord, the "called out," the "chosen"? Repeatedly, it seems. But then, if an edition of the Bible were being written in our day, would such a generalization—the people *"again did evil"*—be appropriate to the people of the Lord, to believers, at this very time?

Because the Lord deals in justice as well as in mercy and because He chastens those whom He loves (see Hebrews 12:6), at times He uses wake–up methods. Judges 4:2 says, "The LORD *sold them* into the hand of Jabin king of Canaan" (emphasis added).* This was not the best of times for the people of God. Verse 3 says, "And for twenty years he harshly oppressed the children of Israel."

In His loving wisdom, the Lord knew how to get the attention of His people. Judges 4:3 relates the results of what He did, "And the children of Israel *cried out* to the LORD" (emphasis added). The harsh treatment that Jabin initiated—the twenty years of oppression—caused the people of Israel to do some reassessing of their relationship with God, and some reexamining of their priorities: "Are the Canaanites becoming 'Israelized,' or are we Israelites becoming 'Canaanized'?"

The next words in the chapter are, "Now Deborah . . ." (verse 4). Then follow verses 6 and 7 and the first mention of Barak. "Then she sent and called for *Barak* the son of Abinoam from Kedesh in Naphtali, and said to

---

*Scripture doesn't say whether that was a matter of His primary will or permissive will.

him, 'Has not the LORD God of Israel commanded, "Go and deploy troops at Mount Tabor; take with you ten thousand men of the sons of Naphtali and of the sons of Zebulun; and against you I will deploy Sisera, the commander of Jabin's army, with his chariots and his multitude at the River Kishon; *and I will deliver him into your hand*"?' " (emphasis added).

The words of the prophet, right? The promise of the Lord, right?

It is so important to remember that God had promised victory: "And I will deliver him [Sisera] into your hand." This is where every victory starts—with God's promises. "By that same mighty power, he has given us all of his rich and wonderful promises. He has promised that you will escape the decadence all around you caused by evil desires and that you will share in his divine nature" (2 Peter 1:4, NLT). Victory—whether over Sisera or whatever else—*begins and ends with God and His promises*! So, "thanks be to God, who gives us the victory through our Lord Jesus Christ" (1 Corinthians 15:57). Yes, God uses Deborahs and Baraks, but the victory—whether for the corporate people of God or for individuals—belongs to God.

Most of us would be thrilled to hear the words of a prophet giving us specific guidance—to say nothing of also giving the marvelous, reassuring promise of victory from the Word Himself! Doesn't it seem that even those with the most "dwarfed" faith among us would be moved, humbled, and privileged to respond to such a revelation of the will of God? One would hope so.

So then, the story of Barak didn't really begin with Barak. It began with Deborah. Barak's response to her sheds both positive and negative light on his character and the strength of his faith. "Barak said to her, '*If you will go with me,* then I will go; but if you will not go with me, I will not go!' " (Judges 4:8; emphasis added).

Let's think positive first. Barak appeared to have a high degree of loyalty to as well as high esteem for the position and office that Deborah held. She said the message she sent him came from the Lord, and Barak accepted it as such without question. Commendable indeed. Mark one down for Barak! Would that all of God's people have such an unhesitating acceptance of the words of a prophet of God, even a modern one.

Barak didn't hesitate because he was questioning whether the message came from the Lord. Rather, he said, "If you will go with me, then I will go; but if you will not go with me, I will not go." Some commentators, such as Adam Clarke, don't see Barak's response as revealing any lack of faith and even cite a remarkable addition to verse 8 that's in the Septuagint version: "Because I know not the day in which the Lord will send his angel to give me success." Regarding this line, Clarke says, "By which he appears to mean, that although he was certain of a Divine call to this work, yet, as he knew not the time in which it would be proper for him to make the attack, he wishes that Deborah, on whom the Divine Spirit constantly rested, would accompany him to let him know when to strike that blow, which he knew would be decisive. This was quite natural, and quite reasonable, *and is no impeachment whatever of Barak's faith.*"[1]

On the other hand

At best, however, it seems that Barak's faith was a tad bit tentative, and his "I'll go if you will" suggests that he had somewhat of a secondary faith when compared to Deborah's more certain, more active faith. I mean, if Deborah hadn't gone to war with him, what part would his faith have played then, and what quality of faith would he have displayed? "I know what You commanded, Lord. I know what You said, Lord. I know what You promised, Lord. But if Deb won't go, I ain't goin' either." Note this commentary on Barak's hesitation: "Although he had been designated by the Lord Himself as the one chosen to deliver Israel, and had received the assurance that God would go with him and subdue their enemies, *yet he was timid and distrustful.*"[2]

So Barak's faith wasn't exactly stellar. Would you call it a conditional faith? Would it not be a faith similar to that of Thomas when he said, "Unless I see in His hands the print of the nails, and put my finger into the print of the nails, and put my hand into His side, I will not believe" (John 20:25)? Is this the kind of faith you admire, covet, and seek? Does it seem like this is the kind of faith that would catapult us into Hebrews 11 status and into eternal salvation in heaven itself?

But did it take faith to do what Barak finally did?

Oh, yes! Look at the passage again.

> Barak now marshaled an army of ten thousand men, and marched to Mount Tabor, as the Lord had directed. Sisera immediately assembled an immense and well-equipped force, expecting to surround the Hebrews and make them an easy prey. The Israelites

were but poorly prepared for an encounter, and looked with terror upon the vast armies spread out in the plain beneath them, equipped with all the implements of warfare, and provided with the dreaded chariots of iron. These were so constructed as to be terribly destructive. Large, scythe-like knives were fastened to the axles, so that the chariots, being driven through the ranks of the enemy, would cut them down like wheat before the sickle.[3]

Judges 4:14 gives us this picture of Barak's faith: "Then Deborah said to Barak, 'Up! For this is the day in which the LORD has delivered Sisera into your hand. Has not the LORD gone out before you?' *So Barak went down from Mount Tabor with ten thousand men following him*" (emphasis added). Again, there's an element of real faith here on Barak's part, and it led him to rout the enemy completely. A total victory. Judges 4:16 affirms this, telling us that "not a man was left" of Sisera's army. I guess when the Lord said, "I will deliver him into your hand," He really meant it!

So, what about 1 John 5:4: "This is the victory that has overcome the world—our faith"? Does God mean this for individual Christians? Can we march out in faith against the enemy with the assurance of 1 Corinthians 15:57: "But thanks be to God, who gives us the victory through our Lord Jesus Christ"? We better believe it!

Whatever measure of faith Barak had, it was enough to lay hold of what God could do, in spite of the odds against his ten thousand men. Judges 4:15 sums it up tersely: "And *the* LORD routed Sisera and all his chariots and his army" (emphasis added). It was God's doing. Barak's faith unleashed God's doing. Judges 5:20 says, "The stars from their courses fought against Sisera." This is called "heavenly help."

Clarke's Commentary enlarges this thought: "The Lord confounded, threw them all into confusion, drove them pell-mell—caused chariots to break and overthrow chariots, and threw universal disorder into all their ranks. . . . There is no doubt all this was done by supernatural agency; God sent his angel and confounded them."[4]

Without detracting from what Barak accomplished for the Lord, the problem is just that he never seemed to be out front with his faith—never seemed to be the faith leader. He was overshadowed by Deborah's position and faith.

Judges 5 seems to confirm this. In some Bible versions, this chapter has the heading "The Song of Deborah and Barak." Did one of them compose the music and the other the lyrics? Did they do a duet? And why did inspiration devote a whole chapter to this song? Why is Barak mentioned only three times in the thirty-one verses when Deborah is mentioned four times? The chapter seems to be primarily a song about Deborah—especially when verse 7 uses the first person to focus on her: "Village life ceased, it ceased in Israel, until I, Deborah, arose, arose a mother in Israel." It seems like Barak is almost an afterthought, an addendum to the song. Almost like, "Oh, I forgot. Barak helped too." But then, Deborah's name isn't mentioned again in the Bible and Barak's is—and it's in Hebrews 11, the faith chapter. So Barak got his due, so to speak.

I don't think it could be said that Barak was a faith giant. But I don't know how many faith giants God actually has. It seems that God works most often through unlikely candidates for the kingdom who have just *some* faith. Is not the grace of God wonderfully magnified in this? And cannot most of us, who have just "a measure of faith," be truly thankful and encouraged that a man like Barak, with his somewhat questionable faith, can end up in Hebrews 11 and also end up saved for all eternity in heaven itself?

---

1. Clarke, *Clarke's Commentary*, 2:117; emphasis added.

2. White, Ellen G. White Comments in *The Seventh-day Adventist Bible Commentary*, 2:1002.

3. Ibid.

4. Clarke, *Clarke's Commentary*, 2:117.

Questions for Reflection and Discussion

1. Why did Barak but not John the Baptist make it into the faith chapter?

2. Would you have chosen Barak to be mentioned in the faith chapter? Why? Why not?

3. Do you think that the "measure of faith" that God has dealt to everyone (Romans 12:3) is enough faith to get us it into the kingdom? Why or why not?

4. Do you think Barak's faith was diminished by his asking Deborah to go with him into battle? Explain.

5. Has it ever been a spiritual goal of yours to have a faith like Barak? Has that changed since you read the preceding chapter? Why or why not?

6. Do you find encouragement in Barak's being listed in Hebrews 11?

7. On page 477 of *The Great Controversy*, Ellen White wrote, "The Christian's life should be one of faith, of victory, and joy in God." How does this apply to Barak? How does it apply to you?

Chapter 7
Gideon, a Good Man, But . . .

Have you ever had the Lord Jesus Christ appear to you in person? Not in a dream. Not in a vision. Not in your imagination. I mean in the flesh.

Have you ever heard Jesus speak to you audibly? I'm not speaking of a "thought voice"; I'm talking about a face-to-face conversation with the Son of God.

Have you ever had the words *The Lord is with you* fall on your ears from the Commander of the heavenly hosts Himself?

I certainly haven't, but Gideon did. He experienced these special privileges and many more.

Gideon. He's known for gaining a great victory over multiplied thousands of Midianites with only three hundred troops.

Who was Gideon?

Yes, Gideon was a warrior. Yes, he commanded the awesome army of three hundred Israelite soldiers. Yes, he delivered Israel from years of grinding oppression by the surrounding enemies. And, yes, he judged Israel for forty years. But who was he?

Bits of information seem to suggest that Gideon was nearing middle age at the time of God's miraculous call. Plus, he may have been a man of means, having many servants and a personal armorbearer.

His name comes from a root word that means "to fell a tree." The name means "feller," or lumberjack, and, by extension, "warrior."[1] According to Judges 6:32, after Gideon tore down an altar of Baal, his father gave him another name, *Jerubbaal*—"let Baal fight" or "let Baal be an adversary." And according to 2 Samuel 11:21, he had a third name, *Jerubbesheth,* meaning "let shame contend." Both of these last-mentioned names seem to highlight his struggle against Baal worship.

Gideon grew up in a home tainted with idolatry. "Gideon's father, Joash, who shared in the apostasy of his countrymen, had erected at Ophrah, where he dwelt, a large altar to Baal, at which the people of the town worshiped."[2] Whether Gideon was influenced by and involved in this flagrant idol worship, we are not told. One commentator suggests that the name *Jerubbaal* means "the enemy of Baal."[3] If this were true, it might denote that Gideon had resisted the example of his father and the corrupting influence of Baal worship, and it might help us to understand better why God used him to fight against the idolatrous enemies that bordered on Israel.

Some authors paint a rather unflattering picture of Gideon.

Who was Gideon? The least considered member of a poor family, of a divided tribe, of which no name was famous in the annals of his country; a man unknown and unheard of, whose occupation was to thresh corn stealthily, lest the Midianites should take it; a man thought nothing of by his own countrymen, and contemptuously overlooked by his foreign masters. *But he was the chosen instrument for delivering Israel.*[4]

He is the youngest scion [offspring] of an insignificant family in a secondary tribe. Not only has he had no special religious or political training, he is an idolater, or at any rate belongs to an idolatrous family.[5]

Not exactly a great résumé. But then, God isn't as interested in a great résumé as He is in willing, obedient hearts. In spite of the fact that Gideon is being listed here as an "unlikely," let us not forget that he did warrant quite a bit of "inspired" press—his calling and his exploits for God occupy chapters 6–8 of the book of Judges. Nor can we ignore the considerable number of positives that characterized his life and experience.

A plethora of positive particulars

Gideon did have an encounter with "the Angel of the LORD"—in fact, several, see Judges 6 and 7. And was this merely an angel or was it God

Himself? We should note that Gideon sensed who the "Angel" really was. He addressed Him as "my Lord" (Judges 6:15), and, more significantly, "Lord God" (verse 22). Ellen White identifies this Angel as Jesus Christ, the Covenant Angel.[6] What an amazing encounter for a nobody like Gideon to have!

On the other hand, how could we possibly label Gideon as a lowly nobody when God addressed him as He did in Judges 6:12, "The Angel of the Lord appeared to him, and said to him, 'The Lord is with you, *you mighty man of valor*' " (emphasis added)? How significant it is that the Lord called him a "mighty man of valor"! Is this not another case in which the Lord looks not upon the outward appearance but on the heart? Was God seeing what Gideon had been in the past or what he was to become in the forty years during which he judged Israel? Whichever it was, it must have been encouraging to Gideon, who was furtively threshing grain and hoping against hope that the Midianites wouldn't notice and come and take his food away.

As *The Pulpit Commentary* expresses it so well: "As long as he thought of himself only as the drudge of the family, a thresher of wheat, a skulker by the wine-press; as long as he felt himself one of a degraded caste, as long as he had no hope, no spirit, no sense of having a mission, he would and could do nothing great. The man, the warrior, the captain, the deliverer, the hero, the martyr, must be aroused within him."[7] So Gideon needed to hear the voice of God addressing him as a "mighty man of valor" to launch him into his God-given role of delivering the people of Israel.

What a wonderfully privileged person he was even to have the Angel of the Lord appear to him at all. But that Angel did more. He came and sat under the terebinth tree and engaged Gideon in conversation. And He told Gideon, "The Lord is with you." As one author has noted, "God knows his servants' true nature and powers. He takes no note of outward appearances. Rank, riches or poverty, family honour, count for little with him. He seeks out the right man wherever he is to be found—at the threshing-floor, by the sheep-fold, in the fishing-boat. God never calls any man to any task for which the man does not possess the requisite talents."[8]

So, God must have seen something in Gideon—some kind of potential there—that led him to address him in that way.

And the positives continued. The Angel commissioned Gideon to save Israel from the Midianites (Judges 6:14). What a calling! What a heavy, heavenly responsibility was entrusted to him!

Then the Angel validated the favor being shown to Gideon with two undeniable miracles.

Judges 6:19–21 tells us that when Gideon brought an offering of meat and bread and put them on a rock, the Angel touched them with the end of His staff, and "fire rose out of the rock and consumed" them. And the second miracle was the famous one involving a fleece, in which the ground was dry at first and the fleece wet, as Gideon had requested, and then the even greater miracle Gideon wanted on the second night—the ground was wet and the fleece was dry.

Also add to these miracles the amazing experience Gideon and his servant Purah had when they crept into the camp of the Midianites and heard the soldiers discussing a dream about their being defeated by Gideon, and then the actual defeat of the Midianites by three hundred of Gideon's men. Gideon was indeed a favored individual whom God used mightily.

Here's a list of the positives:

- The God of heaven spoke to him in person ten times (see Judges 6; 7). Would this not be a coveted contact?
- Gideon manifested faith and obedience in tearing down the altar of Baal (Judges 6:25–27).
- His father called him by a new name, *Jerubbaal*, which meant in effect that he had shown himself to be an enemy of Baal (verses 31, 32).
- After hearing the dream of the Midianite soldier, the first thing Gideon did was to worship (Judges 7:15). He had the right priorities!
- He acted courageously and bravely in taking on "the Midianites and Amalekites and all the people of the East," who were "as the sand by the seashore in multitude" (verse 12), when all he had was three hundred men armed merely with pitchers, lamps, and trumpets (chapter 7).
- When he went into battle, he instructed the three hundred warriors to cry out, "The sword of the LORD and of Gideon!" rather than "The sword of Gideon—O yes, and of the Lord too" (verse 18).
- Ellen White attributed the following characteristics to him: he had "courage and integrity," he was "firm and uncompromising," and he "displayed also a spirit of courtesy that is rarely witnessed."[9]
- He refused the kingship when the people of Israel offered it to him,

saying, "I will not rule over you, nor shall my son rule over you: the LORD shall rule over you" (Judges 8:23). Very commendable, Gideon! A demonstrable nobility.

• He's on the Hebrews 11 faith honor roll.

So, what is there not to like about Gideon? Is there any question about his relationship with God? Isn't it very evident that everything is OK between him and God?

In a way, it might be good if we stopped our examination of his life right at this point, because all of the characteristics listed above are very complimentary of this special person who met a very special need in the history of Israel. And in our hearts, we kind of expect everyone mentioned in Hebrews 11 to be a cut above everyone else—to be faith giants, to be role models of spiritual comportment and attainments. But leaving out the other side of Gideon wouldn't be fair to the picture of God that we're developing or to our understanding of His relationship with us humans. And since the Word has paid more attention to Gideon than to many of his unlikely compatriots, it is important that we examine carefully the whole record of his life.

The not-so-well-known Gideon

We need to go back to the beginning of Gideon's story, when the Angel of the Lord first approached him (Judges 6:11). The first thing the Angel said was "Gideon, the Lord is with you." He then addressed him as a "mighty man of valor."

It does seem that Gideon should have been humbled, impressed, awed, filled with wonderment, be openmouthed, or something when the Angel of the Lord spoke to him. Perhaps he should have fallen on his face. Some say he didn't recognize at that point that he was speaking with an angel— much less *the Angel.* But even the way he was addressed and the fact that the Being was a stranger should have made him realize that this was a very out-of-the-ordinary encounter.

But Gideon was so beaten down, so depressed, so negative, that it all gushed out of him as though a dam had burst. He asked the Angel, "If the LORD is with us, why has all this happened to us? And where are all the miracles our ancestors told us about? Didn't they say, 'The LORD brought us up out of Egypt'? But now the LORD has abandoned us and handed us over to the Midianites" (Judges 6:13, NLT). In other words, "If God is with us, why am I forced to beat out a little wheat in a winepress, of all places, when I should be threshing a huge harvest out in the open fields?" Not a great way to speak to any angel, let alone the Angel.

So, Gideon—this faith-chapter hero—was negative, down-in-the-mouth, whiny, and really pessimistic. How then should we rate his faith at this point? He didn't exactly have a ten-foot-tall faith at the beginning of the story—not that he didn't have cause for discouragement.

In the next verse, all doubt about the stranger's identification is dispelled. God, the Angel of the Covenant, commissioned Gideon. He said, "Go in this might of yours, and you shall save Israel from the hand of the Midianites. Have I not sent you?" (verse 14). God repeated the commission a second time even more forcefully, and He added this promise: "Surely I will be with you, and you shall defeat the Midianites as one man" (verse 16). And what was Gideon's response? Did he say, "Thank You for these strong words of assurance, O God, straight from Your mouth. Your words are powerful and Your promises unfailing, so, relying on Your trustworthiness, I will triumph"? No. He asked for a sign. A sign that the Person speaking to him was really the Angel of the Covenant. A sign that God really meant what He had just said. A just-to-make-sure sign.

Yes, you and I might have done the same thing, but our names aren't in Hebrews 11 and Gideon's name is. He's the one who's supposed to be the model of faith, and asking for signs isn't the surest demonstration of faith.

Are you a "signs" believer? A "signs" Christian, like doubting Gideon and doubting Thomas? If God spoke with you face-to-face and you knew it was God, would you ask for a sign that would convince you that He really meant what He was saying?

God is so sensitive to us, so aware of our needs, so understanding of our humanity, that after He had pared Gideon's army down from thirty-two thousand to three hundred, He knew that Gideon's thin faith would need some bolstering. Note the implication of Judges 7:10, "But if you are afraid to go down . . ." Yes, God knew that Gideon's faith muscles were like wet spaghetti, so in His loving, fatherly tenderness, He gave Gideon a sign that Gideon hadn't even asked for. He told Gideon to take his servant Purah and go down to the Midianite camp, where, through some amazing miracles, he would receive physical therapy for his faith muscles, which would produce immediate results.

To his credit, Gideon did what the Lord asked him to. And when he and his servant drew near to the encampment, they overheard a man talking to his companion. The man said, "I have had a dream: To my surprise, a loaf of barley bread tumbled into the camp of Midian; it came to a tent and struck it so that it fell and overturned, and the tent collapsed" (verse 13).

Scripture says, "Then his companion answered and said, 'This is nothing else but the sword of Gideon the son of Joash, a man of Israel! Into his hand God has delivered Midian and the whole camp' " (verse 14). And when Gideon heard those words, his faith went from flabby to fit, weak to strong—so much so and so fast that the record says "he worshipped." First the fleece, then this affirmation of the Lord's favor, and Gideon became a true believer. But the praise goes to God.

Are we catching the humanity of this man who is included in the faith chapter? The man who was listed along with so many splendid examples? Are we seeing that Gideon was a lot like us in that he wasn't "Mr. Superfaith" but rather "Mr. Averagefaith"—or less? Is it possible that in those circumstances some of us might have had more confidence in God than he did?

"He had many wives"

There's another point about Gideon that we don't need to go into too deeply but that we should at least acknowledge. The Bible says, "Gideon had seventy sons who were his own offspring, for he had many wives" (Judges 8:30). I know about the culture thing, and the time-and-place thing concerning biblical characters and God's dealings with them, but I'm a little uncomfortable with this aspect of the man—and I'm sure some people who are reading this book feel the same way. Our uncomfortableness may well say more about us and our narrow, judgmental thinking than it says about Gideon and the kind of example he was, but it's still there. Undoubtedly, the fact that God chose to include Gideon by name in one of the most exalted chapters in the Bible—many wives or no—says more about our wonderful, accepting God and His all-inclusive love than it does about either Gideon or us twenty-first-century questioners.

Here's another one. This one is perhaps even touchier, but, in fairness, it must be mentioned—because God has mentioned it in His Word. Judges 8:31 says, "His [Gideon's] concubine who was in Shechem also bore him a son, whose name he called Abimelech."

What is it with this concubine?

One commentary enlarges on the question like this: "The sequel indicates that she may have been a Canaanite. The fact that this woman remained with her relatives in Shechem instead of coming to Gideon's home in Ophrah shows that the case was one which the early Arabs called a 'sadika [female friend]' marriage. Under such a marriage arrangement the woman lived with her own people, and was visited by the husband from time to time. The children born to such a marriage were counted as members of the wife's clan, and always lived with the mother."[10]

This doesn't exactly help those of us with a Puritan-like concept of right and wrong and a black-and-white theology about sin and transgressing the law of God. But the sacred record is what it is. For whatever reason, and I choose to believe it was for our encouragement, God decided to use Gideon where he was and as he was. He held him up as an example of faith and obedience in spite of his spiritual shortcomings. And our God doesn't mistake character.

However, for me, the most difficult part of Gideon's being singled out as an example, a faith hero, is what he did as recorded in Judges 8:24–27. *The Clear Word Bible,* although often a loose paraphrase of the Bible, does express the reality and the humanity of the man Gideon quite well.

> Then he [Gideon] said, "I do have one request. I would like each of you to give me one golden earring from your war booty before you leave." It was the custom of the Midianite and Ishmaelite troops to wear such earrings.
>
> They said, "We'll gladly give you these earrings." So they spread out a cloth and everyone threw in the most valuable part of the booty.
>
> The earrings the men gave Gideon weighed forty-three pounds. In addition to this he had taken numerous ornaments and garments from the Midianite kings and gold chains from the necks of their camels.
>
> Gideon praised his men and dismissed them. When he got home he made a vest and a breastpiece from his war booty *like the one the high priest wore.* Then he hung them up in his hometown as a reminder of what the Lord had done for Israel. He also erected an altar there for the Lord, *but he had failed to ask the Lord about these*

things, and they became a spiritual snare to Gideon and his family. The people of Israel abandoned the program of worship Gideon had reinstituted for the Lord and instead worshiped and offered sacrifices to the vest with its breastpiece as if it were an idol.[11]

Ellen White notes, "The unauthorized worship led many of the people finally to forsake the Lord altogether, to serve idols. After Gideon's death great numbers, among whom were his own family, joined in this apostasy. The people were led away from God by the very man who had once overthrown their idolatry."[12]

The war was over. The enemies of God had been defeated. The people of God had been delivered from oppression and slavery. Did Gideon have too much time on his hands? Was his thinking clouded by all his wives and his concubine? Why didn't he seek guidance from the Lord in this matter? How sad that this departure from God's will and God's plan stained the last days of this great faith warrior of God. What a blot on his reputation! At the beginning of his special ministry, he tore down idols that God's people had been worshiping. At the end of his life, he set up an unauthorized something of his own making, which led God's people back into idolatry.

However, there is something that we can't take away from Gideon. Whatever lapses of faith he might have had, whatever weaknesses of character might have surfaced, despite the grievous mistake that caused so many to stumble, he is in Hebrews 11:32. He is home free. Safe. Our God put the "good heaven's keeping" seal of approval on Gideon as an example of faith and faithful obedience.

Was he a Moses, a Daniel, or a Paul? I don't think so. In fact, he belonged to the Six-and-a-Half-Billion Club, like all the rest of us. He was just as human as we are. He was, by all accounts, not the sharpest knife in God's tool drawer. But in spite of Gideon's lapses, inadequacies, and mistakes, God loved him, and He used him, and Gideon will be saved. In telling this story, I'm not trying to lower the standard. I am trying to raise our hopes. Thank You so much, Lord, for the encouragement!

1. Strong, *Strong's Exhaustive Concordance of the Bible,* Hebrew entry 1438, 1439.

2. White, *Patriarchs and Prophets,* 547.

3. Robert Jamieson, A. R. Fausset, and David Brown, *A Commentary Critical and*

Explanatory on the Whole Bible (Grand Rapids, Mich.: Zondervan, n.d.), 162.

4. A. C. Hervey, "Homiletics [on the Book of Judges]," in *Deuteronomy, Joshua & Judges*, vol. 3 of *The Pulpit Commentary*, 61; emphasis added (see "Homiletics" for Judges 6:11–24).

5. A. F. Muir, "Homilies by Various Authors [on the Book of Judges 6:11–15]," in *Deuteronomy, Joshua & Judges*, vol. 3 of *The Pulpit Commentary*, 62 (see homily on Judges 6:11–15).

6. White, *Patriarchs and Prophets*, 547.

7. Hervey, "Homiletics," *The Pulpit Commentary*, 3:62 (see "Homiletics" for Judges 6:11–24).

8. W. F. Adeney, "Homilies by Various Authors [on the Book of Judges 6:11–14]," in *Deuteronomy, Joshua & Judges*, vol. 3 of *The Pulpit Commentary*, 66 (see homily on Judges 6:11–14).

9. White, *Patriarchs and Prophets*, 553, 555.

10. *The Seventh-day Adventist Bible Commentary*, 2:355.

11. Jack J. Blanco, *The Clear Word Bible* (Hagerstown, Md.: Review and Herald®, 1994), 302 (Judges 9:24–27); emphasis added.

12. White, *Patriarchs and Prophets*, 556.

Questions for Reflection and Discussion

1. What effect would a visit by the Angel of the Lord have on your faith?

2. How do you think Gideon's faith compares to Rahab's? Does it really make any difference?

3. Since God appeared to Gideon some ten times, should more have been expected from him than from Barak?

4. What character traits that Gideon had seemed to militate against his faith or possibly "put the lie" to his faith?

5. Would your faith be stronger than it is now if you could witness a couple of direct miracles from God? Why or why not?

6. Compare and contrast the concepts of having faith and being faithful.

7. Are you disappointed by the sins of Gideon? By the sins of others who hold high positions? By yours? If so, how do you gain spiritual equilibrium?

Chapter 8
Samson, the Party Boy

Samson was a big hulk of a man who would surely be considered a real hunk if he were alive today. He was the Arnold Schwarzenegger of twelfth century B.C., a real-life Superman. And his mama named him *Sunshine*—or something like that! A cute little name for someone who may have been the world's strongest man, don't you think? Can you imagine how the kids he grew up with must have teased him?

According to *Strong's Exhaustive Concordance,* the root word behind the name *Samson* meant "to be brilliant; the sun; by impli[cation] the east; . . . ([sun rising])."[1] These meanings remind me of terms that have to do with Jesus Himself. I wonder what Samson's mother was thinking when she named him Sunshine. She and Samson's father must have had very high hopes for their son. And they had a good reason for their high hopes.

The entire thirteenth chapter of Judges is devoted to the events that preceded the birth of Samson. Those events indicate that something special was happening. Scripture notes that

- before Samson's birth, his mother had been barren;
- the "Angel of the LORD" came to give personal instruction to the parents;
- the Angel gave specific dietary instructions for the mother while she was carrying Samson (Judges 13:4);
- Samson was heaven designated to "be a Nazirite to God from the womb" (verse 5);
- the offering Samson's parents made to the Angel was miraculously consumed (verses 15–20);

- and the parents understood that the Angel must have been God Himself (verses 17, 18, 20–22).

So, the pregnancy of Manoah's wife was indeed heaven planned. There can be no question that the instruction the Angel gave came from God. Clearly, Samson was on God's mind—and not only his birth, but his life and mission as well. (What is this thing about a little clump of cells, a "fetus," not being a person?)

Only one thing about Samson's birth disappoints me: his mother's name is never mentioned. She is called "his [Manoah's] wife." She is called "the woman." And one time—only—she is referred to as "his mother" (at least, according to the New King James Version). But we have to consider the times, the culture, and the views of that society on the role of women.

A Samson-planned lifestyle

After Judges 13 and all the amazing events surrounding Samson's birth, the sacred record devotes only one sentence to his growing-up years: "The child grew, and the LORD blessed him" (Judges 13:24). So, we know nothing of how Samson responded to the careful training his parents provided him. Did he feel hemmed in? Did he complain that they were being too strict? Did he act out in rebellion? We don't know because those years are wrapped in silence.

I find it interesting, however, that one of the very first events recorded from Samson's life involved a clash of wills—his parents' and his. It had to do with the extremely important matter of a life companion. Here's the story as told in the New Living Translation:

> One day when Samson was in Timnah, he noticed a certain Philistine woman. [Scripture doesn't say that he'd known her before. He didn't date her. He didn't do any research on eHarmony.com, checking twenty-nine dimensions of compatibility. He didn't talk it over with his parents. He just "noticed" her.] When he returned home, he told [not asked] his father and mother, "I want to marry a young Philistine woman I saw in Timnah." His father and mother objected strenuously, "Isn't there one woman in our tribe or among all the Israelites you could marry? Why must you go to the pagan

Philistines to find a wife?" But Samson told his father, "Get her for me. She is the one I want" (Judges 14:1–3).

I remember a little doggerel that seems appropriate here:

He was warned against the womern—
She was warned against the man.—
But ef that won't make a weddin',
W'y, they's nothin' else that can.[2]

So much for submission to parental authority and listening to good old Mom and Dad!

Samson seemed to have only one criterion as he looked toward marriage: "she pleased Samson well" (Judges 14:7). He came. He noticed. He liked what he saw. Period. Evidently, what Samson wanted, Samson got. Never mind that she was the wrong woman from the wrong background. Never mind that marrying her meant setting aside the inspired admonition forbidding the Israelites to "make marriages with them [the godless tribes in Canaan]. You shall not give your daughter to their son, nor take their daughter for your son" (Deuteronomy 7:3). Never mind the sacred principle that surely was known even before Amos wrote it: "Can two walk together, unless they are agreed?" (Amos 3:3). Evidently, Samson was not only strong of body but also strong of will. That's not good, Samson! Not good.

Ellen White comments, "He did not ask whether he could better glorify God when united with the object of his choice, or whether he was placing himself in a position where he could not fulfill the purpose to be accomplished by his life. To all who seek first to honor Him, God has promised wisdom; but there is no promise to those who are bent upon self-pleasing."[3]

The bachelor party

We also see Samson's self-planned lifestyle in a further departure from God's will as recorded in Judges 14:10, "And Samson gave a feast there, for young men used to do so." Was this the predecessor to the bachelor party held before some weddings today? It's perhaps significant that the Hebrew word translated *feast* means "drink; by impl[ication] drinking."[4] It comes from a primitive root that means "imbibe," or "occasion for drinking."[5] So, this bachelor party was a drinking party. Kind of a party outside of God's will to celebrate the marriage that was outside of God's will. This all fits together with the following observation: "The vale of Sorek was celebrated for its vineyards; these also had a temptation for the wavering Nazarite, who had already indulged in the use of wine, thus breaking another tie that bound him to purity and to God."[6] Departure from God on any point is a slippery slope, isn't it? And for Samson, the slope quickly became steeper.

Judges 14:11 says that when those Samson invited to his party "saw him, . . . they brought thirty companions to be with him." What does that mean? Were these "companions" astonished at Samson's size? Were they awed by his massive muscles? There's no evidence that they were church members, and there *is* every evidence that they were enemies of God's people. Did they feel that they might need some reinforcements to handle this loose cannon of an Israelite if the party got rough? Is that why they brought thirty companions?

At any rate, the party went on—for seven days! At some point early in the feasting, Samson posed a riddle to his thirty guests—maybe because he was flushed with wine, or maybe because he was flushed with his physical prowess, or maybe because this type of thing was done in ancient times. Samson added prizes as incentives: "If you solve my riddle during these seven days of the celebration," he said, "I will give you thirty plain linen robes and thirty fancy robes. But if you can't solve it, then you must give me thirty linen robes and thirty fancy robes" (verses 12, 13, NLT).

You remember the story. They couldn't solve the riddle, so they applied a little subtle pressure on Samson's fiancée to get her to help them. They said, "Get the answer to the riddle from your husband, or we will burn down your father's house with you in it" (verse 15, NLT)!

With this rather powerful motivation, Samson's fiancée used every persuasive tool in her arsenal, including the most potent weapon of all: turning on the tears. After seven days of this, even that man's man Samson was "worn out by her nagging" (verse 17, *The Message*). He told her the answer, she told it to them, and Samson was furious that they had "plowed with [his] heifer" (verse 18). Scripture says that "he went down to Ashkelon and killed thirty of their men, took their apparel, and gave the changes of clothing to those who had explained the riddle" (verse 19).

This story of Samson's quite unspiritual actions doesn't end there. It continues in Judges 15. When he found that his wife had been given to his best man while he was getting the garments, he stormed back to his parents. Then he caught three hundred foxes, turned them tail to tail, put torches between the tails, and let the foxes go in the Philistines' grain fields, burning them up—and their vineyards and olive groves as well.

The Philistines responded by deploying their forces against Judah. Their reason is just what we'd expect from them when Samson had destroyed their fields and their livelihood: "We've come to capture Samson. We have come to pay him back for what he did to us" (Judges 15:10, NLT).

Their explanation was perfectly natural for pagan people. But we might have expected better from Samson when his own people complained to him about the trouble the Philistines were causing them because of what he'd done. However, his answer was pure, broken-down-Nazirite Samsonese: "I only paid them back for what they did to me" (verse 11, NLT). Actually, the contrast is even starker in the New King James Version: "As they did to me, so I have done to them."

Uh, that's not quite what Jesus said. His words were, "Whatever you want men to do to you, do also to them" (Mathew 7:12). Samson wasn't standing on spiritual high ground. It seems like the miraculously born Nazirite should have done better. But Samson was on a roll. Downhill.

More trouble with women

Judges 16 records an episode that began when Samson "spent the night with a prostitute" (verse 1, NLT). Then that chapter moves on to his fateful involvement with Delilah. (Did I mention that she was another Philistine woman?) When, following the orders of the Philistine authorities, she tries to get Samson to tell her the secret of his strength, he lies to her repeatedly. Finally, she gets the truth out of him and then shaves his head, removing the symbol of his strength and power. And one of the saddest, gravest sentences in all of Scripture follows, the direct result of his Samson-planned lifestyle. When for the third time, Delilah yells out, "The Philistines are upon you, Samson!" (verse 20). Scripture says, "He awoke from his sleep, and said, 'I will go out as before, at other times, and shake myself free!' *But he did not know that the LORD had departed from him*" (Judges 16:20; emphasis added). *The Message* says, "He didn't realize that GOD had abandoned him." The New Living Translation says, "He didn't realize the LORD had left him."

Judges 16 gives us the final, dramatic picture of the end of Samson's terribly marred life. He had been summoned to perform in the Philistine temple before the lords and leaders of that country and thousands of its citizens. Samson represented the defeated Israelites. He was a captive, a prisoner, and was blind, his eyes having been put out. He stood there between those massive pillars like a Barnum & Bailey circus attraction.

"Then Samson called to the LORD [this is only the second time Scripture says he prayed], saying, 'O Lord GOD, remember me, I pray! Strengthen me, I pray, just this once, O God' " (Judges 16:28).

His motive for bringing down the temple and killing the several thousand Philistines wasn't exactly noble. He didn't ask for God's help "so more of Your enemies might be destroyed."

It wasn't "so Your people will live safely."

It wasn't "so Your name will be feared in all the nations round about."

It wasn't "so the surviving Philistines will know that You are God and Your name will be honored."

No, his motive was so "I may with one blow take vengeance on the Philistines for *my two eyes*" (verse 28; emphasis added).

Samson could well have had a bumper sticker on his chariot like one I saw on a racy car that an attractive young lady was driving—"It's all about me." *The Seventh-day Adventist Commentary* calls Samson "a spiritual pygmy."[7] And the book *Patriarchs and Prophets* describes Samson in these terms: "Physically, Samson was the strongest man upon the earth; but in self-control, integrity, and firmness, he was one of the weakest of men."[8] How sad that so many of the stories about him justify these harsh characterizations.

So, what did God think of this man who physically was a giant, but spiritually was a ninety-seven-pound weakling? Could He use him? Could He work with him and through him? Could He save him? Could a man like Samson end up in God's kingdom, the home of the "pure and the blest"?[9]

The rest of Samson's story

When so much of Samson's life could be viewed as less than exemplary, doesn't it come as a surprise that he is named in Hebrews' Hall of Fame as a hero of faith? But Hebrews 11:32 does name him—in fact, grouping him with "Gideon and Barak and . . . David and Samuel and the prophets." It's pretty impressive that Hebrews places Samson in the same league as David and Samuel and the prophets. But of course, Hebrews 11 also includes Abraham, Isaac, and Jacob. That it ranks Samson with them is even more impressive.

This chapter goes on to say that all the people it names have "obtained a good testimony through faith" (verse 39). Amazingly, that commendation includes Samson too! And the people listed in Hebrews 11 are going to be in the kingdom. Apparently, that means Samson too. How can this be? On what basis is Samson listed in this chapter as a man of faith and worthy of eternal life? Is God overlooking all of the negatives in his life—all of his failings, all of his willful, deliberate, flagrant sins? Is it right, is it fair, that a man such as Samson should end up in the same place as some of the faith giants such as Enoch and Moses and prophets such as Isaiah and Daniel?

There are points that we need to remember about this strong weakling. In the case of the woman "that pleaseth me," *The Seventh-day Adventist Bible Commentary* says, "Even in this unfortunate marriage God was overruling the course of events for the furtherance of His own designs. He makes even the weakness and poor judgment of men to redound to His praise."[10] Please note that the "overruling" of God is different than His ordering. His permitting is different than His primary willing. We should remember that Samson *did* deliver Israel. Here was an overarching purpose of God at work through Samson. What he was to accomplish was foreseen, planned for, yes, *ordained* in the mind of God. The sins Samson committed, the way he chose to do things, his willful, selfish acts—God didn't ordain these. But the deliverance that Samson wrought (by God's blessing and power) was in the heart and mind and will of God.

It is important that we remember also the last sentence of Judges 16:31, "He [Samson] had judged Israel for twenty years." Samson's judging of Israel must not have been all bad, all the time. God must have used him repeatedly during those years.

Notice also how often Scripture says the Spirit of God used him.

- Judges 13:25, "And the Spirit of the LORD began to move upon him."
- Judges 14:6, "And the Spirit of the LORD came mightily upon him."
- Judges 14:19, "Then the Spirit of the LORD came upon him mightily."
- Judges 15:14, "Then the Spirit of the LORD came mightily upon him."

These expressions stand even though we may not understand the relationship between the Spirit of the Lord coming upon him and his tearing the lion apart; his going to Ashkelon and killing thirty men; or the ropes becoming like flax, his bonds breaking loose from his hands, and his finding of a fresh jawbone of a donkey and killing a thousand men with it. Who of us can fathom, let alone dictate, what one might do when the Spirit of the Lord comes upon a chosen vessel? Even regarding his visiting a harlot, *Patriarchs and Prophets* says, "Notwithstanding his sin, God's mercy had not forsaken him."[11]

But note this telling statement from that same book: "God's promise that through Samson He would 'begin to deliver Israel out of the hand of the Philistines' was fulfilled; but how dark and terrible the record of that life which might have been a praise to God and a glory to the nation! Had Samson been true to his divine calling, the purpose of God could have been accomplished in his honor and exaltation. But he yielded to temptation and proved untrue to his trust, and his mission was fulfilled in defeat, bondage, and death."[12] We should also remember this powerful sentence: "In suffering and humiliation, a sport for the Philistines, *Samson learned more of his own weakness than he had ever known before; and his afflictions led him to repentance.*"[13]

Giants of faith

After Judges 16:31, which speaks of his burial, Samson isn't mentioned in the Bible again—until Hebrews 11:32, where he's listed among the giants of faith! What kind of grace is this? What kind of mercy? What kind of forgiveness? What kind of salvation?

Samson was an imperfect man, a sinner; often failing, falling, stumbling; frequently setting a bad example; over and over again showing a proclivity for doing his own thing and misrepresenting his God and his calling. And yet God chose him, called him, put him in a position of leadership, strengthened him, repeatedly put His Spirit upon him, and finally elected him to faith's Hall of Fame.

So, does this prove that we can sin and still live rather than die? Does it prove that lifestyle makes no difference? Does it prove that God doesn't place a premium on obedience? Does it prove that God just winks at sin? None of the above. But it does prove that God can work with us wherever we are spiritually. He calls and uses imperfect people. He accomplishes His purposes through us in spite of ourselves. He can't use holy, righteous, mature people who never sin because there are none. God does His work through less-than-perfect vessels.

The Seventh-day Adventist Bible Commentary notes, "The experience of Samson indicates that God does not immediately forsake His servants when they fall into sin. He may continue to bless their efforts, even though they are living in conscious disregard of some specific requirement of God. Inasmuch as no one is without fault, God would be unable to use human instrumentalities in His work, if He could bless only the efforts of the sinless. Since this is true, no one should interpret the blessings of heaven as proof that God approves of all his deeds."[14]

For us to take license from the sins of Samson, believing that we also will make it into faith's Hall of Fame and be saved at last, would be terribly presumptuous and perhaps eternally fatal. However, from Samson's story we can take new hope in the love and mercy of God and new courage from His desire for "all men to be saved" (1 Timothy 2:4). This is the will of God for all who would look and learn from this unlikely candidate for the kingdom of heaven.

---

1. Strong, *Strong's Exhaustive Concordance,* Hebrew entry 8121. Or *Samson* might mean "destroyer," but it doesn't seem likely that Samson's mother would have tagged him with such a negative name.

2. James Whitcomb Riley, "On a Splendud Match," in *Neighborly Poems and Dialect Sketches* (Indianapolis, Ind.: Bobbs-Merrill Co. Pub., 1897), 71.

3. White, *Patriarchs and Prophets,* 563.

4. Strong, *Strong's Exhaustive Concordance,* Hebrew entry 4960.

5. *The Seventh-day Adventist Bible Commentary,* 2:389.

6. White, *Patriarchs and Prophets,* 565.

7. *The Seventh-day Adventist Bible Commentary,* 2:394.

8. White, *Patriarchs and Prophets,* 567.

9. W. H. Hyde, "We Have Heard," in *The Seventh-day Adventist Hymnal* (Hagerstown, Md.: Review and Herald®, 1985), no. 453.

10. *The Seventh-day Adventist Bible Commentary,* 2:388.

11. White, *Patriarchs and Prophets,* 565.

12. Ibid., 567.

13. Ibid., 566; emphasis added.

14. *The Seventh-day Adventist Bible Commentary,* 2:390.

Questions for Reflection and Discussion

1. On a scale of 1–10, how would you rate Samson's faith?

2. What implications does Samson's death have regarding suicide?

3. What implications does Samson's life have regarding the Christian lifestyle?

4. Does the story of Samson cause you any problems?

5. Do you think it's fair that Samson is included in Hebrews 11, the faith chapter? Why or why not?

6. Do you think heaven will have a large number of Samson-like saints? Why or why not?

7. Why is it and how is it that God can use us when we are Samson-like?

Chapter 9
Solomon, the Wisest Foolish King

What a stellar beginning! Even before Solomon was born, the stars were shining for him. In a sense, he was a son of promise, and it was God Himself who did the promising. He told David, "When you die, I will raise up one of your descendants, and I will make his kingdom strong. He is the one who will build a house—a temple—for my name. And I will establish the throne of his kingdom forever. I will be his father, and he will be my son. If he sins, I will use other nations to punish him. But my unfailing love will not be taken from him as I took it from Saul, whom I removed before you" (2 Samuel 7:12–15, NLT). No wonder Ellen White said, "His early life was bright with promise."[1] How could he go wrong? How could this man ever become an unlikely candidate for the kingdom?

Solomon's name appears in Scripture nearly three hundred times. He's mentioned ten times in the New Testament—twice by Jesus Himself. Solomon was inspired to write parts of three of the thirty-nine books of the Old Testament—Proverbs, the Song of Solomon, and Ecclesiastes. Only Moses, Paul, and John wrote more books of the Bible than Solomon did. And 1 Kings 4:32 says he wrote three thousand proverbs and one thousand and five songs—certainly a God-inspired accomplishment.

It was David, his father, who named him *Solomon*, which means "peaceful."[2] Matthew Henry, a Bible commentator, says, "They called him *Solomon—peaceful*, because his birth was a token of God's being at peace with them, because of the prosperity which was entailed upon him, and because he was to be a type of Christ, the prince of peace."[3] Solomon was David and Bathsheba's second son. Their firstborn, the son of their adultery, became ill and died shortly after birth. So, God's favor, which followed His judgment, seemed an indication to them that they were in God's peace and in

God's grace once again. Can we not all testify that God's gracious bestowals continue even after we have sinned?

If there was any doubt about the bestowal of God's favor upon David and Bathsheba after their sin, it was all erased when God Himself gave a special name to Solomon. That name appears only one time, in 2 Samuel 12:25, "He sent word by the hand of Nathan the prophet: So he called his name Jedidiah, because of the LORD." Is this special? Very much so, because *Jedidiah* means "Beloved of the LORD."

God said of Jesus, "This is My beloved Son" (Matthew 3:17). Five times Scripture calls John the apostle "the disciple whom Jesus loved." And God Himself named Solomon *Jedidiah*, "Beloved of the LORD." Would it not be a massive understatement to say this is good company for Solomon to be in?

Scripture testifies repeatedly that during Solomon's early years, he was a model king.

- First Kings 3:3: "Solomon loved the LORD, walking in the statutes of his father David."
- First Kings 3:5–9: God appears to Solomon and gives him a blank check. Solomon asks for only one thing: "an understanding heart." What restraint! What humility! Then God gives him everything he asked for and everything else he could have asked for but didn't, including riches and honor unparalleled!
- First Kings 9:2: "The LORD appeared to Solomon the second time." God's personal contact—not once, but twice. Wouldn't any of us settle for once?
- Second Chronicles 1:1: "Solomon the son of David was strengthened in his kingdom, *and the LORD his God was with him and exalted him exceedingly*" (emphasis added).
- Nehemiah 13:26: "Among many nations there was no king like him, who was beloved of his God." The accolades and the affirmations never seem to stop coming.
- Second Samuel 12:24: "Now the LORD loved him." OK! OK! Solomon was God's pet!
- Jesus mentions Solomon on two occasions, citing his glory, wisdom, and greatness (Matthew 6:29; 12:42).
- First Chronicles 29:25 puts the exclamation point to Solomon's

hardly imaginable beginnings: "Solomon rode high on a crest of popular acclaim—it was all God's doing. God gave him position and honor beyond any king in Israel before him" (*The Message*).

Inspired commentary continues the "bright with promise" insights into those untainted early years.

- "For many years he walked uprightly, his life marked with strict obedience to God's commands."[4]
- "The name of Jehovah was greatly honored during the first part of Solomon's reign."[5]
- "As the years went by and Solomon's fame increased, he sought to honor God by adding to his mental and spiritual strength, and by continuing to impart to others the blessings he received."[6]

Endless possibilities, a future unlimited. A "smoking the tires" start. So favored by God! So loved by God! What perfect plans God had for Solomon. How could those plans possibly fail?

Descent into "unlikeliness"

If only the story and the record of Solomon stopped at the end of 1 Kings 10, after his marvelous witness to the Queen of Sheba.

If only Adam and Eve hadn't fallen into a wretched state of "unlikeliness" and lostness.

If only Saul had obeyed the word of God through Samuel.

If only the life of David hadn't included the unimaginable sins of lust and murder.

If only Peter hadn't denied Christ with ugly, foul, fisherman's oaths.

If only the "if onlys" weren't a part of the human condition. But, sadly, every life seems to have its share of them—Solomon's certainly not the exception! Praise God that He knows about, has planned for, and has the cure for the "if onlys"!

The dark side of the life of Solomon starts in 1 Kings 11:1, which begins with the word *But*. In that text, the use of this word conveys an almost inspired wistfulness, a hesitancy to go on. "But King Solomon loved many foreign women." And "many" was by no means an overstatement. First

Kings 11:3 says there were seven hundred of them. And, oh yes, did I mention the three hundred concubines he also kept?

Was this a problem or something?

It was, on several counts. God's plan, His model marriage, comprises one husband and one wife. Further, many of Solomon's wives were "from the nations of whom the LORD had said to the children of Israel, 'You shall not intermarry with them, nor they with you' " (1 Kings 11:2). God had kindly given warnings about this course of action: "Surely they will turn away your hearts after their gods" (verse 2). God, in His omniscience, gives no empty, frivolous warnings and cautions. What the record goes on to say demonstrates this: Solomon's "wives turned away his heart. For it was so, when Solomon was old, that his wives turned his heart after other gods; and his heart was not loyal to the LORD his God, as was the heart of his father David" (verses 3, 4).

The broad road that leads to destruction is numbing and mesmerizing. Ellen White says, "So gradual was Solomon's apostasy that before he was aware of it, he had wandered far from God. Almost imperceptibly he began to trust less and less in divine guidance and blessing, and to put confidence in his own strength. Little by little he withheld from God that unswerving obedience which was to make Israel a peculiar people, and he conformed more and more closely to the customs of the surrounding nations."[7]

Solomon's rationalizations, as he started downward, were airtight.

- Political and commercial alliances with other nations (made, in part, through marrying their women) will bring to these nations the knowledge of God. (Sure they will!)
- My wisdom and my power and my example will lead these foreign wives to the worship of the true God. (Right!)
- Finally, I know that some of these things I'm doing are outside of God's will and against His law, but think of how many other peoples and nations will be exposed to who God really is.

Solomon's course away from God is proof positive that all of us have our PhDs in rationalization.

Scripture itself speaks starkly about Solomon's headlong descent into the lust of the flesh, the lust of the eyes, and the pride of life.

Solomon took up with Ashtoreth, the whore goddess of the Sidonians, and Molech, the horrible god of the Ammonites.

Solomon *openly defied* GOD; he did not follow in his father David's footsteps. He went on to build a sacred shrine to Chemosh, the horrible god of Moab, and to Molech, the horrible god of the Ammonites, on a hill just east of Jerusalem. He built similar shrines for all his foreign wives, who then polluted the countryside with the smoke and stench of their sacrifices.

GOD was furious with Solomon for abandoning the GOD of Israel, the God who had twice appeared to him and had so clearly commanded him not to fool around with other gods. Solomon faithlessly disobeyed GOD's orders.

GOD said to Solomon, "Since this is the way it is with you, that you have no intention of keeping faith with me and doing what I have commanded, I'm going to rip the kingdom from you and hand it over to someone else" (verses 5–11, *The Message;* emphasis added).

And little wonder that God disciplined him. After all, he erected an idol to which living children were offered as sacrifices! These snippets of quotations paint the picture in somber, dark reality.

- "From the wisest and most merciful of rulers, he degenerated into a tyrant. Once the compassionate, God-fearing guardian of the people, he became oppressive and despotic."[8]
- "He mistook license for liberty. He tried—but at what cost!—to unite light with darkness, good with evil, purity with impurity, Christ with Belial."[9]
- "Raised to a pinnacle of greatness and surrounded with the gifts of fortune, Solomon became dizzy, lost his balance, and fell."[10]
- "So complete was his apostasy, so hardened his heart in transgression, that his case seemed well-nigh hopeless."[11]

O Jedidiah, Jedidiah! What happened to the glorious morning of your reign? O "Beloved of the LORD," you were warned about multiple wives and political alliances and giving your devotions to other gods. How could you? O Solomon, your beginnings were so bright with promise and your potential to glorify the name of Jehovah was brighter still. Why, oh why? O son of promise, how could your momentous wisdom morph into monumental foolishness?

Some human beings start out as total unlikely candidates for the kingdom. Others start off well but then drive themselves into the brick wall or over the precipice or into the flames of unlikeliness. Such was Solomon! By his choices, his unconscionable actions, and the resultant horrible consequences, he ran away with the title of imbecile king of tenth century B.C. Hands down! Nobody close!

His name, "Beloved of the LORD"; God's promise to David that He would establish the kingdom of his son; the gift of God that Solomon asked for, and all of the extravagant gifts that God gave him in addition: was this all for nothing? And what about his kingdom candidacy now?

Blessed are the "unlikelies."

Really?

The possibility of his salvation

John the revelator penned these words: "To Him who loved us and washed us from our sins in His own blood, and has made us kings and priests to His God and Father, to Him be glory and dominion forever and ever. Amen" (Revelation 1:5, 6). There are reasons enough to believe that King Solomon will be among those kings and priests who ascribe glory and honor and praise to the King of kings Himself forever and ever. You see, God, being the kind of God He is, doesn't have to have a lot of reasons to be able to save us in His kingdom.

Second Peter 3:9 continues the thought. It says that God "is longsuffering toward us, *not willing that any should perish but that all should come to repentance*" (emphasis added). Isaiah wrote, "The LORD will wait, that He may be gracious to you; and therefore He will be exalted, that He may have mercy on you" (Isaiah 30:18). And the message God instructed Ezekiel to pass on encourages all the unlikelies: "Say to them: 'As I live,' says the Lord GOD, 'I have no pleasure in the death of the wicked, but that the wicked *turn from his way and live*. Turn, turn from your evil ways! For why should you die, O house of Israel?' " (Ezekiel 33:11; emphasis added). And the God of all grace and mercy repeats these words again and again. God isn't into excluding people from His kingdom but rather into including all whom He can. The God whom Solomon first worshiped is in the saving business, not the losing business.

Remember, Solomon wrote parts of three important books of the Bible: Proverbs, Ecclesiastes, and the Song of Solomon. "Jewish tradition asserts that Solomon wrote Song of Solomon in his youthful years, Proverbs in his middle years and Ecclesiastes in his latter years. This book may be expressing his regret for his folly and wasted time due to carnality and idolatry."[12] There are commentators aplenty who see the last two verses of Ecclesiastes 12:13, 14 as evidence of Solomon's repentance, godly sorrow, turning back to the Lord, and coming to his senses toward the close of his life:

Let us hear the conclusion of the whole matter:

> Fear God and keep His commandments,
> For this is man's all.
> For God will bring every work into judgment,
> Including every secret thing,
> Whether good or evil.

Ellen White described his last days this way: *"The Lord forsook him not.* By messages of reproof and by severe judgments, He sought to arouse the king to a realization of the sinfulness of his course." Again: "Awakened as from a dream by this sentence of judgment pronounced against him and his house [1 Kings 11:14–28], Solomon with quickened conscience began to see his folly in its true light. Chastened in spirit, with mind and body enfeebled, *he turned wearied and thirsting from earth's broken cisterns, to drink once more at the fountain of life. For him at last the discipline of suffering had accomplished its work."*[13]

Yes, Solomon disobeyed.

Yes, he set aside all of God's warnings.

Yes, he failed to rule his own passions.

Yes, he committed unthinkable acts of idolatry.

Yes, he built an image to a pagan god to whom children were sacrificed.

Yes, his example led many to eternal loss.

But listen! "None who have fallen need give up to despair. . . . If they repent, forsake sin, and turn to God, there is still hope for them. . . . God hates sin, but He loves the sinner. 'I will heal their backsliding,' He declares; 'I will love them freely.' Hosea 14:4."[14]

Solomon couldn't undo the dishonor he had shown toward God nor the damage he had done to the people of God and the nation.

But neither could Adam and Eve.

Neither could Manasseh.

Neither could the apostle Paul.

There is good reason to believe that Solomon did turn around spiritually; that he did come back. He wrote out his record of sin and folly but also the record of his repentance. And Inspiration records that "Solomon's repentance was sincere."[15]

Scripture says that there will be some who will be saved "as by fire" (1 Corinthians 3:15, KJV). Solomon may be one of those. But in the kingdom, not one of the redeemed will hear the words, "Say, I've noticed that you smell a little smoky." If a person is saved for all eternity, that person is saved—period! And if a person is in the kingdom of God, that person is there! And are there not varying degrees of unlikeliness in all of us?

1. White, *Prophets and Kings,* 25.

2. Strong, *Strong's Exhaustive Concordance,* Hebrew entry 8010.

3. Matthew Henry, "Second Samuel XII," in *Joshua to Esther,* vol. 2 of *Commentary on the Whole Bible* (Grand Rapids, Mich.: Christian Classics Ethereal Library, 2000), http://www.ccel.org/ccel/henry/mhc2.iiSam.xiii.html; emphasis in original.

4. White, *Prophets and Kings,* 27.

5. Ibid., 32.

6. Ibid., 33.

7. Ibid., 55.

8. Ibid., 55, 56.

9. Ibid., 58.

10. Ibid., 68.

11. Ibid., 75.

12. Introductory notes on the book of Ecclesiastes in *The New Open Bible, Study Edition,* New King James Version (Nashville: Thomas Nelson Publishers, 1990), 746.

13. White, *Prophets and Kings,* 77; emphasis added.

14. Ibid., 84.

15. Ibid.

Questions for Reflection and Discussion

1. When the sins of King Saul and King Solomon were so similar, so grievous, and so flagrant, why did God's treatment of the two men differ so?

2. Which dominated in Solomon's life, his being an unlikely candidate for the kingdom or a likely candidate?

3. How well does Solomon's life illustrate the long-suffering of God?

4. Using Solomon and his life, discuss why it is not only impossible, but also terribly wrong for us to judge other people at any point in their lives.

5. What are your feelings about someone who is so high yet falls so low?

6. What do you consider to be the most amazing part of Solomon's life?

7. Do you think that God lowers His standard by having people like Solomon in His kingdom?

Chapter 10
Notable Naaman

What's notable about Naaman? Not that much, really. Only that

- he had position and power as commander of the army under King Benhadad II in Syria;
- he was steeped in everything the world has to offer;
- he was a "heathen";
- he worshiped the sun god;
- he had warred against and defeated Israel;
- he had a pride that wouldn't quit;
- and he had a volatile temper.

There's only one other person with the name *Naaman* in the entire Bible so there is no confusion about who this Naaman was. The one in whom I'm interested here is mentioned in only one chapter in the Old Testament—2 Kings 5—and one verse in the New Testament—Luke 4:27. That's all.

A great biography

Second Kings 5:1 introduces us to Naaman: "Now Naaman, commander of the army of the king of Syria, was a great and honorable man *in the eyes of his master,* because by him the LORD had given victory to Syria. He was also a mighty man of valor, but he was a leper" (emphasis added). However, the story of Naaman isn't so much about who he was as it is about who he became— how the Lord sought him, helped him, healed him, and converted him.

Naaman was a notable personage, no doubt about that. Benhadad II was one of the greatest Syrian kings, and Naaman had helped him gain that reputation by leading Syria's army to victory over their enemies, among whom was the northern kingdom of Israel. However great Naaman was in his own right, though, the lowest slave in Syria probably wouldn't have traded places with him, because Naaman was a leper, and in those days, leprosy was the kiss of death.

As to Naaman's religious background, while there is no direct statement, 2 Kings 5:15, 18 implies that he may have been a worshiper of Rimmon. Barnes's commentary notes, "Rimmon is known to us as a god only by this passage. The name is connected with a root 'to be high.' Hadadrimmon Zechariah 12:11, the name of a place near Megiddo, points to the identity of Rimmon with Hadad, who is known to have been the Sun, the chief object of worship to the Syrians."[1]

Immediately after introducing Naaman and his leprous condition, the story in 2 Kings tells us about the young Israelite girl who served—"waited on"—Naaman's wife (2 Kings 5:2). It seems a raiding band had captured her and brought her back to Syria. Whoever this girl's parents were and whatever her background, something about her religion, her God, the faith of Israel, and her own personal faith had stuck in her heart, because she had the temerity to say, "If only my master were with the prophet who is in Samaria! For he would heal him of his leprosy" (verse 3). What a testimony from a young girl! It's amazing that she would put herself out on a limb in such a serious matter.

It's even more amazing that Naaman actually acted on this young girl's advice. Something about her must have given him a glimmer of faith in what she said—and in her God. And it's more amazing still that when Naaman told Benhadad, the king, what this young girl had said, he believed as well. What was there about her life, her service, her conduct, that caused Naaman to accept her suggestion so readily? He believed because the girl believed—what a powerful testimony for witnessing! Wasn't it a God thing that this young lady came into Naaman's household? Didn't God look into the heart of this great and good man and see that no matter how unlikely he seemed, he would be a true believer if only he had some light?

When did God start seeing "likelihood" in an unlikely heathen who was the commander of an army? It must have been before the Syrian raid into northern Israel. Did the God of heaven direct the leader of that Syrian raiding party as to where to enter the Israelite territory? Had the Lord been thinking in eternity past about this chain of events that would lead Naaman into the faith of Israel, toward the God of Israel, and into the kingdom of God itself? Yes, indeed! Of course!

What a marvelous testimony to the mind-boggling truth of Isaiah 46:3, 4, "I created you and have cared for you since before you were born. I will be your God throughout your lifetime—until your hair is white with age. I made you, and I will care for you. I will carry you along and save you" (NLT). The God of the universe had his eye on Naaman before Naaman was born—before Naaman ever gave Him a thought. And this is only an illustration of how He fixes on, focuses on, every single individual of the billions who have inhabited this planet. But we're getting ahead of our story.

The first nineteen verses of 2 Kings 5 are all about Naaman. The last eight verses are mostly about Gehazi, Elisha's servant-coworker. Isn't it amazing? One unlikely individual coming *to* the light, and one seemingly likely candidate for the kingdom turning away *from* the light! One exchanging his leprosy for health and healing and salvation, and the other exchanging his wholeness and hope for the physical leprosy and the "sin leprosy" that threatened to keep him from the kingdom.

Put one down for Naaman. Some God-given spark of faith burst into flame so that he immediately acted on the words of a Hebrew servant girl. He immediately contacted the king. The king was all for the possibility of his commander-servant's healing and immediately had a letter composed, asking the king of Israel to make it happen. And evidently Naaman immediately left carrying the letter and many thousands of dollars' worth—some say millions of dollars' worth—of gifts to "buy" his healing. Health care wasn't inexpensive back then either!

A glitch or two

However, as with most stories and life experiences, there were some glitches, some roadblocks. The first occurred when the king of Israel read Benhadad's letter, "Now be advised, when this letter comes to you, that I have sent Naaman my servant to you, that you may heal him of his leprosy" (2 Kings 5:6). Exploding with consternation, the king—probably Joram, the son of Ahab—tore his clothes at what he considered to be an act of provocation. He thought that Benhadad was charging *him* with the task of taking away Naaman's leprosy. The king of Israel said, "This man sends me a leper to heal! Am I God, that I can kill and give life? He is only trying to find an excuse to invade us again" (verse 7, NLT). Perhaps he was thinking of his father Ahab and a similar request that he had received as a pretext for war against Israel.

Instead of taking the responsibility upon himself, Joram might have thought of Elisha, the prophet whose miracle-working powers were un- doubtedly widely known. But he thought only of himself, forgetting there was a prophet in Israel. However, the story of his rending his kingly gar- ments quickly spread around the area and reached Elisha himself. Stories and rumors do spread quickly!

Elisha's response was God-centered rather than self-centered. He sent Joram a message: "Please let him [Naaman] come to me, and he shall know that there is a prophet in Israel" (verse 8). Elisha was anxious for God to be glorified in Syria through the healing of Naaman. God wants us ever to remember that He doesn't care for and have plans for believers only, but for unbelievers as well. "Unlikelies," if you please.

Evidently, Naaman wasn't deterred by the king's horrified reaction. When Elisha's message reached Joram, "then Naaman went with his horses and chariot, and he stood at the door of Elisha's house" (verse 9). The sec- ond glitch happened at this point—one that was more serious than the first. It could have sabotaged the whole beautiful experience.

The Bible doesn't say that Naaman knocked on Elisha's door or that trumpets announced his arrival, but Elisha must have heard the commo- tion and known that Naaman had arrived. However, instead of going to the door and acknowledging Naaman's presence, his office, and the importance of his personage, Elisha remained inside and sent a messenger. A lesser fig- ure. The message from the prophet was simple and direct: "Go and wash in the Jordan seven times, and your flesh shall be restored to you, and you shall be clean" (verse 10).

Elisha hadn't acknowledged Naaman's station, his importance, his of- fice, or even his presence. Surely, God had communicated to Elisha about all of this. Surely He must have had a reason for having Elisha treat Naa- man so. It must have been a test of Naaman's faith.

Anyway, it was too much for the proud heathen commander. "Naaman lost his temper. He turned on his heel saying, 'I thought he'd personally come out and meet me, call on the name of GOD, wave his hand over the diseased spot, and get rid of the disease. The Damascus rivers, Abana and Pharpar, are cleaner by far than any of the rivers in Israel. Why not bathe in them? I'd at least get clean.' He stomped off, mad as a hornet" (verse 11, *The Message*).

Naaman's pride was causing him to rebel against the command from the prophet of God. Scripture says he "went away" (verse 11). We don't know how far he went, but at the least, he was in the act of leaving. He had wanted recognition. He had wanted drama. Elisha coming out. Bowing. Scraping. VIP treatment. And all he got was an order to go to the Jordan and dip in its muddy waters seven times. He was offended and indignant because of the shoddy treatment he had received. *What!* he thought. *Aren't our rivers in Damascus better than the Jordan—in water that looks like coffee grounds?* And so, Scripture says, "he turned and went away in a rage" (verse 12).

Naaman commanded the army of the kingdom of Syria. He was a trusted advisor of the king. He had the respect of his troops and of the Syrian people in general. These weren't exactly reasons for humility—haughtiness maybe, but not humility.

Naaman's pride brought him so close to missing the cleansing. So close to missing the kingdom. He was standing at a crossroad of faith. Would it be his way or God's way?

His servants saved him from the rash consequences toward which his anger was pushing him. Speaking deferentially, they said, "My father, if the prophet had told you to do something great, would you not have done it?" (verse 13). And reason prevailed. Naaman's pride humbled, he did it—he obeyed. The reward? "His flesh was restored like the flesh of a little child, and he was clean" (verse 14). And as quickly as Naaman was healed of the death-dealing leprosy, so quickly was his heart healed from the most death-dealing disease of all—sin.

Did Naaman say, "Hallelujah!"? We don't know. Did he raise his hands to heaven with words of thanksgiving and praise? Scripture doesn't say. Did he kneel on the banks of the Jordan in recognition of and humble submission to the only true God? We haven't a clue. What we do know is that Naaman and all his aides went back to Elisha's house. We do know that he stood before the prophet. And we do know that he uttered this profound confession of faith: "I know at last that there is no God in all the world except in Israel" (verse 15, NLT). Matthew Henry's commentary says, "He had formerly thought the gods of Syria [to be] gods indeed, but now experience had rectified his mistake, and he knew Israel's God was God alone, the sovereign Lord of all. Had he seen other lepers cleansed, perhaps the sight would not have convinced him, but the mercy of the cure affected him more than the miracle of it. Those are best able to speak of the power of divine grace who have themselves experienced it."[2]

How long does it take to go from being lost to being in a saving relationship with the God of heaven? From heathen to God-worshiper? From eternal separation *from* God to eternal fellowship *with* God? From nearly impenetrable darkness to blinding, beautiful, saving light? One miracle? One epiphany? One aha? One teachable moment?

A genuine conversion

Are we jumping to conclusions about Naaman's salvation? Is it a stretch to believe that he became and remained a confirmed candidate for the kingdom? There are powerful reasons to believe that he did.

First, God gave Naaman the opportunity to express his faith by his actions, and then He granted the desire of Naaman's heart. This certainly was some kind of marvelous, miraculous manifestation of the goodness of God, the approval of God, and the acceptance of God.

Second, Naaman came back to thank Elisha. Interesting, isn't it, that a Syrian leper did this in Old Testament times and so did one of the ten lepers whom Jesus healed in New Testament times—"and he was a Samaritan" (Luke 17:16)? Jesus commended the Samaritan for his returning to give thanks, and added, "Arise, go your way. Your *faith* has made you well" (verse 19; emphasis added). Might He not have said something similar to Naaman had He been present in the flesh when Naaman returned to Elisha's house?

Third, Naaman most certainly professed his new faith. "I know at last that there is no God in all the world except in Israel." This is remarkably similar to Nebuchadnezzar's faith declaration hundreds of years later, after Daniel had miraculously revealed his dream to him. "The king answered Daniel, and said, 'Truly your god is the God of gods, the Lord of kings' " (Daniel 2:47). And Naaman declared his faith in front of all of his aides.

Fourth, Naaman had it in his heart to give Elisha a huge gift—an offering, if you please. Giving gifts to God's servants and to His cause is one of the evidences of a change of heart and a change of direction.

Fifth, there's that response of Naaman that sounds strange to us: "Please allow me to load two of my mules with earth from this place, and I will take it back home with me. From now on I will never again offer burnt offerings or sacrifices to any other god except the LORD" (2 Kings 5:17, NLT).

One Bible commentary says of this verse,

> What was his motive or his purpose was in this proposal, whether he thought that God could be acceptably worshipped only on his own *soil*, or he wished, when far away from the Jordan, to have the *earth* of Palestine to rub himself with, which the Orientals use as a substitute for water; and whether, by making such a request of Elisha, he thought the prophet's grant of it would impart some virtue; or whether, like the modern Jews and Mohammedans, he resolved to have a portion of this *holy earth* for his nightly pillow, it is not easy to say. It is not strange to find such notions in so newly a converted heathen.[3]

It sounds like Naaman was trying to "do it right"!
Ellen White says that after the miracle Naaman was a new man.

- "Naaman, a heathen nobleman, had been faithful to his convictions of right, and had felt his great need of help. He was in a condition to receive the gifts of God's grace. He was not only cleansed from his leprosy, but blessed with a knowledge of the true God. . . . Thus even the heathen who choose the right as far as they can distinguish it are in a more favorable condition than are those who have had great light and profess to serve God, but who disregard the light, and by their daily life contradict their profession."[4]
- Naaman was a man "upon whose mind had broken a wonderful light, and who was favorably disposed toward the service of the living God."[5]

It's a great confirmation of the continuing faith of Naaman that Jesus mentioned him. He said, "Many lepers were in Israel in the time of Elisha the prophet, and none of them was cleansed except Naaman the Syrian" (Luke 4:27). How significant this mention by the Savior Himself! In telling the story of Naaman, Elisha, and the unnamed servant girl, Ellen White notes Jesus' reference to Naaman: "Centuries after Naaman returned to his Syrian home, *healed in body and converted in spirit,* his wonderful faith was referred to and commended by the Saviour as an object lesson for all who claim to serve God."[6]

The only uncertainty about Naaman's conversion and the likelihood of his candidacy for the kingdom is another request he made of Elisha just before he returned to Syria. *The Clear Word Bible* paraphrase takes the liberty of adding to Scripture, but perhaps it does capture the intent of Naaman's request: "May the Lord God of Israel forgive me for one thing. When King Benhadad goes into the temple of the god Rimmon, he asks me to go with him so he can lean on my arm for he is old and unsteady on his feet. When he bows before his god I have to bow with him, *but I won't do it to worship.* May the Lord forgive me for this."[7]

Elisha's response, "Go in peace" (verse 19), seems to suggest no shadow of doubt lay on Naaman's being a believer. In fact, these words appear to be Elisha's blessing on Naaman. Could it be that he was saying, "God will be all right with that, Naaman. He'll understand because He knows your heart and your motives"? Or was he just giving a new believer some room to grow? We can't know for sure, but Jesus' implied commendation of Naaman seems to leave no room to doubt that this unlikely man who was the commander of the Syrian army did indeed become a credible, likely candidate for the kingdom of heaven.

1. Albert Barnes, *Notes on the Bible,* http://barnes.biblecommenter.com/2_kings/5.htm (see commentary on 2 Kings 5:18).

2. Henry, "Second Kings V," in *Joshua to Esther,* vol. 2 of *Commentary on the Whole Bible,* http://www.ccel.org/ccel/henry/mhc2.iiKi.vi.html.

3. Jamieson, Fausset, and Brown, *A Commentary Critical and Explanatory on the Whole Bible,* 233; emphasis in original.

4. White, *The Desire of Ages,* 239.

5. White, *Prophets and Kings,* 252.

6. Ibid.; emphasis added.

7. Blanco, *The Clear Word Bible,* 459 (2 Kings 5:18); emphasis added.

Questions for Reflection and Discussion

1. Why did God offer healing to Naaman and not to any of the Israelite lepers who lived during the ministry of the prophet Elisha?

2. Does God have a different set of kingdom requirements for a heathen military officer such as Naaman as opposed to a person such as Samuel who literally grew up in the church?

3. What might Naaman's witness have looked like back in his own nation, in his old haunts, and in the presence of all the royal extravagance and the evil of a heathen kingdom?

4. What early fruits of the Spirit, of change, and of conversion appeared after Naaman's healing?

5. Is it easier for a person who has less light and less knowledge to become a likely candidate for the kingdom than for one who has more light and more knowledge?

6. The story we've been considering in this chapter doesn't end where we did. It goes on to tell about the greed of Gehazi, Elisha's servant, and the consequent sentence he received of becoming leprous himself. Do you think that in addition to becoming a leper, he lost his eternal life?

7. What kind of encouragement is there for us in Naaman's story? How might we understand God better from this story?

Chapter 11
Jonah, a Not-so Minor Prophet

One traveler observed that among all the patriarchs, prophets, and others whose features appear on the ceiling of the Sistine Chapel, beyond all question the most beautiful and most notable is that of Jonah. Even in the artwork the early Christians traced on the walls of the catacombs, the most familiar figure is Jonah. He is certainly one of the best-known characters of the Bible—along with the whale (better, the "large fish") in which he resided for three dark, dank, smelly days.

However, the only place Jonah is mentioned in the Bible other than the book that goes by his name is 2 Kings 14:25, which says that Jeroboam II "restored the territory of Israel from the entrance of Hamath to the Sea of the Arabah, according to the word of the LORD God of Israel, which He had spoken through His servant Jonah the son of Amittai, the prophet who was from Gath Hepher." Biographical information about him is virtually nonexistent. That's true of his father Amittai too.*

The introduction of Jonah in his book places him squarely in the category of the unlikelies: "Now the word of the LORD came to Jonah the son of Amittai, saying, 'Arise, go to Nineveh, that great city, and cry out against it; for their wickedness has come up before Me.' But Jonah arose to flee to Tarshish from the presence of the LORD. *He went down to Joppa . . .*" (Jonah 1:1–3; emphasis added).

In the Bible, there are twelve so-called minor prophets. Jonah is one of them. Certainly, Amittai's son wasn't an Isaiah, Jeremiah, Ezekiel, or Dan-

---

*We don't know for sure who wrote the book of Jonah. The book doesn't state that Jonah was the author, and it tells Jonah's story in the third person. But the traditional view has been that Jonah was the author. See *The Seventh-day Adventist Bible Commentary,* 4:995.

iel. But he *was* a prophet of God, a spokesperson for God nonetheless, and that isn't a minor position.

When God confronts a human being

We're introduced to Jonah at a point in his life when the word of the Lord confronts him. Perhaps this is where our own stories start, too, for everything else in our lives is of secondary importance to our response when God and His Word confront us. It's at this point that we see our real selves. It's at this point that we reach a crossroad of decision. We face an either-or. God's will or our will. And something of eternity hangs on the decision we make.

Jonah could have thought all day, but he couldn't have come up with anything he wanted to hear less than God's words: "Arise, go to Nineveh." This command contained something new for a prophet of God—not that God never before commissioned one of His prophets to pronounce judgments upon heathen nations, but previously it had always been a long-distance pronouncement. Long distance is comfortable. Face to face isn't. And God was asking Jonah to go into the heart of a powerful heathen nation and to broadcast the hopeful, helpful, encouraging message that "yet forty days, and Nineveh shall be overthrown" (Jonah 3:4)! And the command was inescapable.

Why would Jonah hesitate when God's instructions were so simple? So straightforward? So unmistakable? There were a lot of reasons.

- Nineveh was a long distance away, and there were no planes, trains, or automobiles—and, most likely, not even a chariot in which Jonah could ride. A donkey perhaps? Five hundred miles was a long, hard trip in Jonah's day.
- The sheer size of the city was overwhelming. Nineveh was no Gath Hepher, Jonah's hometown. It was at the height of its splendor at that time, with walls forty feet thick and sixty feet high. The most important, imposing city of its day.
- The spiritual climate in Nineveh was formidable and off-putting. The city was filled with idolaters and with everything else ungodly. Nahum 3 describes the city's wickedness at one point. Verse 1 starts off with "Woe to the bloody city! It is all full of lies and robbery,"

and verse 4 calls Nineveh "the seductive harlot, the mistress of sorceries."

- Of course, there is the minor factor that Jonah was probably deathly afraid.

However, there was one more overriding reason Jonah was reluctant to go and feared going. It doesn't show up until the fourth and final chapter of the book. In verse 2 of that chapter, Jonah finally admits why he didn't want to go to Nineveh in the first place: "God! I knew it—when I was back home, I knew this was going to happen! That's why I ran off to Tarshish! I knew you were sheer grace and mercy, not easily angered, rich in love, and ready at the drop of a hat to turn your plans of punishment into a program of forgiveness!" (*The Message*).

Jonah was afraid that his mission would be successful! He was afraid the Ninevites would repent, and he feared that then God would change His mind about destroying them. And how would this prophet from Gath Hepher look when what he warned was going to happen didn't happen? People would think he was a fake! Besides, if God was going to destroy Nineveh, why couldn't He just go ahead and do it without telling the wicked people who lived there about it? If they were ready to be destroyed, they were ready to be destroyed—and anyone could see that was the case!

To say that Jonah *wanted* the Ninevites to be destroyed wouldn't misrepresent his motives. It seems plain that he had the same spirit as James and John did when they asked Jesus, "Lord, do You want us to command fire to come down from heaven and consume them?" (Luke 9:54). Jonah didn't want to look like a fool or a liar. He wanted to look good. So, why him? Why now? Why there? Oh, there were plenty of reasons and questions.

Jonah's downside

When Jonah "arose to flee to Tarshish," there was absolutely no question about what he was doing. Jonah 1:3 makes it abundantly clear that he was fleeing "from the presence of the LORD." This phrase is used three times between verses 3 and 10, so it isn't a matter of speculation. We're looking at a deliberate act of disobedience. Jonah didn't want to face God and deal with His very clear directions. He knew what the assignment was, and he knew who gave it. There was no misunderstanding here.

Jonah's running away from God was a resolute revolt. Deliberate disobedience. He couldn't excuse himself by saying, "Did You really mean, Lord, that You actually wanted me to go to Nineveh?"

The more Jonah thought about the command of the Lord, the more negative his reaction became, and the more determined his resistance. Ellen White wrote, "While he hesitated, still doubting, Satan overwhelmed him with discouragement."[1] So, Tarshish instead of Nineveh.

Perusing a map of that part of the world provides some interesting insights. Jonah lived in Gath Hepher, about three miles from Nazareth. Nineveh was about five hundred miles to the northeast, and Joppa one hundred miles in the opposite direction, to the southwest. Furthermore, Tarshish, Jonah's intended destination, was some twenty-two hundred miles to the west of Gath Hepher—about as far from Nineveh as people of that time and place could imagine going! Do you get the idea that Jonah really didn't want to do what God asked him to do?

I can almost see Jonah walking down the waterfront in Joppa and checking to see where the different ships were sailing.

"Could you tell me where you're headed?"

"We're headed for Tyre on the evening wind."

That wouldn't do. Tyre was a hundred miles north. Jonah moves on to the next ship.

"Going on a long voyage?"

"We're sailing to Egypt."

"Oh. That's not far enough."

Eventually, in answer to Jonah's inquiry, one of the sailors says, "We're bound for Tarshish." Scripture says, "So he paid the fare" (Jonah 1:3).

The New Open Bible's introduction to the book of Jonah observes, "Of all the people and things mentioned in the book—the storm, the lots, the sailors, the fish, the Ninevites, the plant, the worm, and the east wind—only the prophet himself fails to obey God."[2]

Jonah really worked at getting lost. And, of course, there's always a price to pay for going in the opposite direction from God's will and command. In the context of some of the reasons Jonah was disobeying the Lord, *The Pulpit Commentary* says that these considerations "would have had small influence had his heart been right."[3] It's so tempting to go in the opposite direction of God's will when our hearts aren't right.

On top of being disobedient, Jonah had an anger problem. Jonah 4:1 says, "It displeased Jonah exceedingly, and he became angry." What was this about?

It was about what chapter 3, verse 10, says happened in Nineveh: "God saw their works, that they turned from their evil way; and God relented from the disaster that He had said He would bring upon them, and He did not do it."

Jonah, the prophet of God, was angry, really angry, at God because of His mercy toward the thousands of people who lived in Nineveh. That's exactly what Jonah had feared would happen. He was really upset that the Ninevites were spared. He was exceedingly displeased that they had repented and diverted the doom they deserved. He felt God changing His mind and His plan put him in a bad light as a prophet. It made him look like a false prophet, untrustworthy, not worth his pay.

Seeing this "man of God," this divinely appointed evangelist to Nineveh, so displeased at the results of his campaign makes me feel sad. One hundred twenty thousand sinners had responded to his message. They had chosen to repent and change their ways. They were hoping that Jonah's God would change His mind and take into account their genuine sorrow for their wickedness. All this because of the message the prophet-evangelist had delivered. And he was bemoaning the results! He was angry at God for being so soft—angry that the destruction hadn't actually occurred. So angry that he wanted to die. He actually prayed about it. "O Lord," he said, "please take my life from me, for it is better for me to die than to live" (Jonah 4:3). What kind of a prophet was this petulant and self-centered man?

To make matters worse, Jonah went through the "pity party" thing all over again. God grew a plant that gave Jonah some shade as he sat outside the city while watching to see what might happen, hoping that fire would yet fall. But, the next day, the plant died and the sun beat down on Jonah's head so that he grew faint. Then once more he wanted to die.

The Lord tried to reason with him. He said, "Is it right for you to be angry about the plant?" (verse 9).

Unbelievably, this poor prophet answered, "Yes . . . even angry enough to die!" (verse 9, NLT). The finite Jonah says to the infinite God, "Yes, I do have a right to be angry. In fact, I have every reason to be exceedingly upset with You, with the Ninevites, with my mission, with the outcome, and with this plant that died leaving me in the sun. Just kill me."

"How different the circumstances of this prayer, compared with that of ch. 2 [when he was inside the great fish], and how different the spirit that prompted it! There he prayed for life; here, for death. There he was humble; here, he is angry."[4]

Through the whole mostly sad story, we see the mercy of God for a wicked, but repenting people, and the mercy of God for a not-so-stellar prophet who seems to fit comfortably into the unlikely category.

The God's-eye view

It isn't difficult to point out the unlikely aspects of someone's character—certainly Jonah is no exception. However, we can't ignore a God's-eye view of Jonah—the good points, his faith, the lessons learned, the obedience rendered (although somewhat forced), the mighty results that his preaching produced. We see the obvious mistakes and weaknesses; God sees into the mind and heart and motives. We judge by what's on the outside; God takes into account what's inside. We form our opinions with limited knowledge; God weighs all the factors—birth, heredity, environment, upbringing—and does so righteously and justly, with an incredible love for every individual. Jonah was a prophet. He was a spokesperson for the only true God. God had called him to this high office. He saw something to use, something to bless, and something to save for eternity.

When the sailors were at their wits' end because of the storm, throwing their cargo overboard to lighten the load, fearful for their lives, and, finally, casting lots to see whose fault it was that they were in this precarious position, Jonah acted like a man. He didn't try to hide his disobedience. And when the sailors asked him, "What shall we do to you that the sea may be calm for us?" he took full responsibility for his actions and said, "Pick me up and throw me into the sea; then the sea will become calm for you. For I know that this great tempest is because of me" (Jonah 1:11, 12).

Remember, Jonah didn't know about the fish yet or the miraculous deliverance or the mercy of God. His book wasn't in the scriptural scrolls yet, so he hadn't read it. He was sacrificing himself for the good of these godless sailors. He was willing to die to make things right so that the crew could be saved. Isn't there some Christlikeness here?

Jonah's manliness in accepting the blame for the predicament of all those on the ship and the calm that followed when the pagan sailors threw him overboard had a powerful effect on everyone there. "Then the men feared the LORD exceedingly, and offered a sacrifice to the LORD and took vows" (verse 16). Did this experience affect the rest of their lives? Did God use this change point to touch the lives of their family and friends? Will some of those sailors be in the kingdom because of Jonah's selfless act? We don't know.

However, we do know what 1 John 3:16 says, "By this we know love, because He laid down His life for us. And we also ought to lay down our lives for the brethren." Isn't this what Jonah did? And didn't he reflect what Paul wrote about the Savior: "In due time Christ died for the ungodly" (Romans 5:6)? Jonah sacrificed himself on behalf of the ungodly sailors just as Jesus sacrificed Himself for the ungodly human race.

Jonah was also a praying prophet. Some might diminish the impact of this fact by saying, "Well, who wouldn't pray if they were in the belly of a whale* with seaweed wrapped around their heads?" Nevertheless, the prayer Jonah prayed is a beautiful and meaningful one.

"I cried out to the LORD because of my affliction,
And He answered me.

"Out of the belly of Sheol I cried,
And You heard my voice.
For You cast me into the deep,
Into the heart of the seas,
And the floods surrounded me;
All Your billows and Your waves passed over me.
Then I said, 'I have been cast out of Your sight;
Yet I will look again toward Your holy temple.'
The waters surrounded me, even to my soul;
The deep closed around me;
Weeds were wrapped around my head.
I went down to the moorings of the mountains;
The earth with its bars closed behind me forever;
Yet You have brought up my life from the pit,
O LORD, my God.

---

*Actually, Scripture calls the creature that swallowed Jonah a "great fish" (Jonah 1:17), but since "Jonah and the whale" is so familiar, I've stuck with the whale throughout this chapter.

"When my soul fainted within me,
I remembered the LORD;
And my prayer went up to You,
Into Your holy temple.

"Those who regard worthless idols
Forsake their own Mercy.
But I will sacrifice to You
With the voice of thanksgiving;
I will pay what I have vowed.
Salvation is of the LORD."

It seems what Jonah did might be called praying through one's problem. In the darkness, in the belly of a whale, Jonah discovered righteousness by faith. There was no question in his mind that he was totally dependent on God for any kind of salvation or deliverance—a lesson we can learn without a whale or any other kind of disciplinary action. But the point is that Jonah did learn it. "At last Jonah had learned that 'salvation belongeth unto the Lord.' Psalm 3:8. With penitence and a recognition of the saving grace of God, came deliverance."[5]

Jonah was mightily used of God in two instances. He sacrificed himself for the stricken, desperate sailors, and their lives were saved. And he preached to thousands in Nineveh, and they repented, and their doom was averted. No other person in Scripture had results like those, which Jonah's preaching produced. Perhaps Peter's preaching at Pentecost comes to mind, when three thousand souls were baptized in one day. But, by the power of God, Jonah brought the entire city of Nineveh to repentance. Ellen White wrote, "Their doom was averted, the God of Israel was exalted and honored throughout the heathen world, and His law was revered."[6] This change lasted for many years. No evangelist, ancient or modern, has ever been used so mightily or experienced such striking results from his preaching.

Reasons to believe Jonah will be there

Because Jonah was born on this sinful planet, he had negative qualities that displayed his humanness, his unlikeliness. This side of his character disappoints us. *But even at best,* God has only earthbound, falling, failing sinners to work with and through. For several reasons we can believe it likely that Jonah will be in the kingdom.

- It seems unlikely that any of the Bible authors won't make it into the kingdom.
- While the story of Jonah opens with his singularly willful disobedience, the second chapter shows how, albeit under discipline, he remembered the Lord in his difficulty, how he cried out to the Lord, how the Lord granted his prayer and delivered him, and how he discovered the essence of salvation.
- When God gave Jonah a second chance, he obeyed. "So Jonah arose and went to Nineveh, according to the word of the LORD" (Jonah 3:3). If Christ "became the author of *eternal salvation* to all who *obey* Him" (Hebrews 5:9; emphasis added), could He not have authored eternal salvation for Jonah?
- Through Jonah, God effected one of the most powerful revivals in history. Jonah was an instrument of God. He was blessed of God.
- Hebrews 11 doesn't contain Jonah's name, but he still might be part of that chapter. After mentioning sixteen examples of faith, the author of Hebrews declares, "The time would fail me to tell of . . . *the prophets*" (Hebrews 11:32; emphasis added). Couldn't Jonah be in that group? Why not give him the benefit of the doubt?

It's too bad that the story of Jonah ends the way it does. It shows him as small and petty, in another fit of anger, and again wanting to die. But his story tells us that God watches over unlikelies. God is long-suffering with unlikelies. God uses and blesses unlikelies. God saves unlikelies who at some point do a 180-degree turn, discover where salvation really is, and obey the Word of God. Like Jonah!

---

1. White, *Prophets and Kings,* 266.

2. Introductory notes on the book of Jonah in *The New Open Bible, Study Edition,* New King James Version, 1029.

3. H. D. M. Spence and Joseph S. Exell, eds., introduction to the book of Jonah in *Amos to Malachi,* vol. 14 of *The Pulpit Commentary* (Grand Rapids, Mich.: Eerdmans, 1950), i.

4. *The Seventh-day Adventist Bible Commentary,* 4:1006, 1007.

5. White, *Prophets and Kings,* 269.

6. Ibid., 271.

Questions for Reflection and Discussion

1. What do you think would have happened if, instead of telling the sailors to throw him overboard, Jonah had said, "Take me back to Joppa—I'm supposed to be going to Nineveh"? What if he had said, "I'll pray and ask God to forgive me and to stop this storm"?

2. In your opinion, why did Jonah tell the sailors to throw him overboard? What was good about that? What was bad about it?

3. Is the sin of Jonah in fleeing much different from the sin of Gehazi in lying to Naaman?

4. At what point might you be like Jonah in fleeing from a direct command of God?

5. How is the character of God exalted in the story of Jonah?

6. Do you consider Jonah to be a man of God?

7. Do you consider Jonah likely or unlikely to be in the kingdom?

Chapter 12

Nebuchadnezzar, the King Who Gained Two Crowns

The whole story could hardly be more unlikely. Why it hasn't been made into a box-office-sellout movie is hard to understand.

The story of Nebuchadnezzar, king of Babylon, is filled with conquering armies, bloody battles, lust for power, ruthless murder, unbridled ambition, unimaginable wealth, breathtaking intrigue, nail-biting suspense, over-the-top decadence, unbelievable miracles, and seemingly impossible outcomes. And drop into this planet-in-rebellion milieu the themes of God (King of kings; Ruler over all) and teenage Jewish hostages, who would rather die than transfer their allegiance from their God to the greatest earthly monarch of that age, and you have an amazing, fairy-talelike picture that is all true.

So, what about this king whose name—either Nebuchadnezzar or Nebuchadrezzar—appears ninety-one times in eighty-eight verses of the Sacred Record? Isn't he a most unlikely candidate for the kingdom of heaven?

A less than heavenly bio

Yes, there were positives about Nebuchadnezzar. He wasn't some minor king. Ellen White calls him "the greatest ruler of the age."[1] And *The Seventh-day Adventist Bible Commentary* offers these evaluations of him: "Nebuchadnezzar was outstanding among the kings of antiquity."[2] He "was the Neo-Babylonian Empire personified."[3] He was "the genius of the Gentile world. . . . Eminently wise, and [having] an innate sense of justice and right. He was, in fact, the leading personality of the Gentile world."[4] Even God pointed to his prominence, calling him "the mighty one of the heathen" (Ezekiel 31:11, KJV).

And yes, Nebuchadnezzar had reason for a measure of pride because he poured his energy and intensity into making Babylon, his capital city, one of the wonders of the world. Ellen White referred to it as "the chief glory of his kingdom, 'the golden city,' 'the praise of the whole earth.' "[5]

According to an ancient record, Nebuchadnezzar said, "[From] the Upper Sea [to] the Lower Sea (one line destroyed) . . . which Marduk, my lord, has entrusted to me, I have made . . . the city of Babylon to the foremost among all the countries and every human habitation; its name I have [made/elevated] to the (most worthy of) praise among the sacred cities."[6]

So, what made King Nebuchadnezzar an unlikely candidate for heaven?

Well, to begin with, he was heathen born and heathen reared and heathen trained. Oh, gods certainly were involved in his upbringing—just not *the God*. Nebo and Marduk were his gods, and both of them were no gods. And he ruled over an idolatrous people, who were just like him.

True, the prophet Daniel miraculously interpreted one of his dreams (recorded in Daniel 2). And "for a time afterward, Nebuchadnezzar was influenced by the fear of God; but his heart was not yet cleansed from worldly ambition and a desire for self-exaltation. The prosperity attending his reign filled him with pride. In time he ceased to honor God, and resumed his idol worship with increased zeal and bigotry."[7] Nebuchadnezzar didn't exactly grow up singing "Jesus loves me, this I know." Nor was he in Pathfinders, and he didn't go to church school or attend either Babylon Adventist Academy or Babylon Adventist University.

One of the seven deadly sins is pride, which God hates. It was front and center in Nebuchadnezzar's experience. In just three paragraphs in one of his inscriptions, he uses the *I* word thirteen times. In the final sentence, he says, "I ere[cted there] a stela (showing) me (as) everlasting king."[8] This certainly wouldn't qualify as a statement of humility, and the attitude he displayed there is hardly a passkey into the heavenly kingdom.

There's also the well-known passage in Daniel 4:28–31, which is paraphrased so graphically in *The Clear Word Bible*. In that passage, Nebuchadnezzar, in his own words, goes on display as the king of pride:

> After Belteshazzar [Daniel's Babylonian name] interpreted the dream, this is what happened to me, King Nebuchadnezzar of Babylon. About a year later, as I was strolling in the roof garden of my palace, I looked out over the city and said to myself, "What a beautiful sight! I'm the one who built this magnificent city! I'm the

one who put this nation on its feet and made it into a great empire! It was my intelligence and power that did all this, no one else's. This great Babylon will stand as a monument to me forever."[9]

Very few people can handle a large serving of power, position, pomp, fame, and wealth without developing a majorly inflated ego, and as you can see, Nebuchadnezzar wasn't among the few.

Other characteristics of the king that place him among the unlikelies were his royal impatience and his ironfisted temper. In the Daniel 2 story of the dream he had, his wise men, astrologers, fortune-tellers, sorcerers, magicians, and wizards couldn't tell him what his dream was and what it meant. They said, in a rather impolitic way, that his demands were unfair. "There isn't a man alive who can tell Your Majesty his dream! And no king, however great and powerful, has ever asked such a thing of any magician, enchanter, or astrologer! This is an impossible thing the king requires. No one except the gods can tell you your dream, and they do not live among people" (Daniel 2:10, 11, NLT).

Nebuchadnezzar wasn't used to being played with, put off, or stalled. And were they saying that His Majesty was unreasonable or something? That, according to different translations, "set the king off. He lost his temper" (Daniel 2:12, *The Message*). He became "angry and very furious" (KJV), "flew into a rage" (TEV). Some might say, "He went ballistic." Did Nebuchadnezzar have an unrighteous anger problem or something? Would anger-management counseling have solved that problem? You could tell he was upset. "He sent out orders to execute all the wise men of Babylon" (verse 12, NLT). He didn't waste time with courts, trials, judicial process, and so forth. He just said, "Kill them!"

Changing the divine prophecy

Nebuchadnezzar's unlikeliness appears again in Daniel 3. He had made an impressive image of gold and commanded all the officials in all his provinces to come to the dedication he planned for it. In the dream of the image recorded in Daniel 2, the one Daniel interpreted, the head of gold represented Nebuchadnezzar. In other words, he was merely one part of the image, and the silver, bronze, and iron kings and kingdoms would succeed him and his kingdom. But Nebuchadnezzar would have none of that. No king would be greater than he was. No kingdom would supplant Babylon. So he made the entire image of gold. The whole amazing statue was 100 percent Nebuchadnezzar, and 100 percent Babylon.

Let me give the king credit where credit is due. According to Ellen White, it was the wise men of his kingdom who suggested that he broadcast his position as the head of gold. It was they who suggested that he have an image like the one in his dream manufactured and then set it up where everyone could see it and see the head of gold that represented him and his kingdom.

Ah, but it was Nebuchadnezzar who loved the idea, and it was he who took it a giant step further by deciding to make the whole image of gold. Why not? It would be "symbolic throughout of Babylon as an eternal, indestructible, all-powerful kingdom, which should break in pieces all other kingdoms and stand forever."[10]

Forget Daniel's interpretation. Forget the stone that smashed the image and destroyed all the kingdoms it represented. Forget that it was the coming kingdom of Christ that would last forever. No. No! It was his kingdom that would smash the others. His kingdom that would last forever. And "with an enthusiasm born of boundless ambition and selfish pride," he would usurp the position of Christ Himself.[11]

It hadn't been that long ago that Nebuchadnezzar was acknowledging the God of heaven for who He is, "Truly your God is the God of gods, the Lord of kings" (Daniel 2:47). But he had a lot of lessons to learn about God and about himself.

The impression that Nebuchadnezzar's inspired dream made on him, which prompted his remarkable acknowledgment, didn't last long. And the divine portrayal of kingdoms that would succeed him didn't set well with him either. Not only was he unimpressed, but he was also defiant. He seemed to think, *God may be good at revealing dreams, but He's not so good at predicting the future, because my kingdom, my Babylon, will last forever.*

And when Daniel's three friends refused to bow down to the golden image, humiliating Nebuchadnezzar in front of all the top brass in the Neo-Babylonian Empire, he flew into a rage and had them brought before him. Demonstrating his magnanimous nature, he gave Shadrach, Meshach, and Abed-Nego a second chance to bow down to his golden image, but the offer included an insolent thrust at God: "And who is the god who will deliver you from my hands?" (Daniel 3:15). A truly Pharaoh-like response of defiance.

When the three Hebrew worthies once again refused to turn their backs on *the* God and worship a "no god," Nebuchadnezzar went into an insane fury and his face became distorted with rage. There is no evidence that insane fury is a fruit of the Spirit. Mindlessly, Nebuchadnezzar blurted out an order that the fiery furnace be heated seven times hotter. (Wouldn't a fiery furnace operating at its normal temperature be hot enough to consume the three recalcitrants?) The uncommitted heart, the unrenewed heart, under the control of the prince of darkness and given the right provocation, is capable of splendid irrationality.

Even when the God of heaven miraculously delivered the faithful young men from the seven-times-hotter fire, Nebuchadnezzar's unregenerate nature—the human nature that made him an unlikely candidate for the kingdom—manifested itself in kind of a stunning reversal. He now decreed "that any people, nation, or language which speaks anything amiss against the God of Shadrach, Meshach, and Abed-Nego shall be cut in pieces, and their houses shall be made an ash heap; because there is no other God who can deliver like this" (verse 29). A laudable acknowledgment of God—accompanied by a high-handed decree based on brute force and cruelty. Not very compatible.

Despite Nebuchadnezzar's deep state of unlikeliness, God was so merciful to him, so patient with him—as He is with us—that over and over again He revealed Himself to this heathen king and gave him opportunity after opportunity to seek a crown that would last forever. We can see that when we take another look at those stories.

Towards becoming a kingdom candidate

To begin with, Nebuchadnezzar didn't realize it, but the God of heaven was loving him, seeking him, gifting him, planning for him long before he even gave God a thought. That's God's default *modus operandi*—His normal mode of operation. It's just what He does.

Jeremiah 27:5–7 reveals this. It shows how God was guiding and gifting Nebuchadnezzar: "I have made the earth and all its people and every animal. I can give these things of mine to anyone I choose. Now I will *give* your countries to King Nebuchadnezzar of Babylon, *who is my servant*. I have put everything, even the wild animals, under his control. All the nations will serve him and his son and his grandson until his time is up" (NLT; emphasis added).

Daniel himself made the king aware of the real God when he told him, "You, O king, are a king of kings. For the God of heaven has *given you* a kingdom, power, strength, and glory; and wherever the children of men dwell, or the beasts of the field and the birds of the heaven, He has given them into your hand, and has made you ruler over them all" (Daniel 2:37, 38; emphasis added).

Nebuchadnezzar's first brush with the God of heaven came when Daniel and his companions were examined by the king and found to be "ten times better" (Daniel 1:20) than all of his "wisdom czars." There was something about these men. They were different. They seemed to be surrounded by an aura of wholesomeness. They had some kind of otherworldly atmosphere about them. Nebuchadnezzar would come to learn that they were standouts for God.

And then God, through Daniel, opened Nebuchadnezzar's dream book and not only told him what he dreamed but what it meant.

The magicians couldn't do it.

The astrologers didn't have a clue.

The sorcerers couldn't tell him.

The Chaldeans couldn't, even though they "were the foremost astronomers of their day" and had been schooled "in other exact sciences, such as mathematics."[12] And on top of all of their skills and knowledge, those wise men added the dubious, devilish machinations of magic and astrology. Still, not only could they not interpret the king's dream, but they also didn't know what it was.

But the God of heaven knew what the dream was. He had given the dream to Nebuchadnezzar! And the God of heaven knew what the dream meant as well. He was about to unveil the future to the king—"the latter days" (Daniel 2:28). And the God of heaven was about to introduce Himself to Nebuchadnezzar and make an impression upon him that would last . . . for a short time.

God would do all of this through His humble, faithful, courageous servants: Daniel and his companions. And He would do it because their lives were at stake. He would do it because the first thing they did when a humanly impossible challenge confronted them was to go to God in prayer. A prayer meeting seeking the One who knows all about dreams and visions and the thoughts of every person on the planet.

And God honored their faith and their prayers. "The secret was revealed to Daniel in a night vision" (verse 19). Then follows the rehearsal of the dream and the interpretation in one of the simplest, clearest, most classic prophecies of the whole Bible.

So was Nebuchadnezzar impressed? Were his eyes opened? Did he meet God?

When Daniel finished, "King Nebuchadnezzar bowed to the ground before Daniel and worshiped him, and he commanded his people to offer sacrifices and burn sweet incense before him. The king said to Daniel, 'Truly, your God is the God of gods, the Lord over kings, a revealer of mysteries, for you have been able to reveal this secret' " (verses 46, 47, NLT).

Was the king just rolling out some flowery phrases? Or did the miracle move him deeply?

"Then the king appointed Daniel to a high position and gave him many valuable gifts. He made Daniel ruler over the whole province of Babylon, as well as chief over all his wise men. At Daniel's request, the king appointed Shadrach, Meshach, and Abednego to be in charge of all the affairs of the province of Babylon, while Daniel remained in the king's court" (verses 48, 49, NLT).

Nebuchadnezzar was impressed! However, no one has been able to determine exactly how much time passed between Daniel 2 and 3, so we aren't sure how long this amazing introduction to the God of heaven continued to shape the king's thinking and actions.

God introduces Himself again

Please know that our God doesn't give up on us easily. He's divinely patient and persistent. He pursues. He allures. He prompts. He taps us on the shoulder. He gives us not just one chance but many chances—as long as there's a possibility that we might yield to His love. He is, as a poet has portrayed him, "the Hound of heaven"—relentless in His pursuit of us. And Nebuchadnezzar needed another introduction.

The image was all of gold this time. Nebuchadnezzar assembled all the officials of his kingdom and demanded that they bow down in worship to the image of himself. But Daniel's three friends stuck to their wonderfully courageous determination not to worship any god other than the only true God. The king, in his insane anger, had them thrown into the fiery furnace. And then the unexpected. Enter the "form of the fourth" in the midst of the flames (Daniel 3:25). Not just Shadrach, Meshach, and Abed-Nego, but another figure. Four in the fire. A fourth one . . . "like the Son of God" (verse

25). Would this incredible miracle make a believer out of Nebuchadnezzar? Would this undeniable, inexplicable happening turn his heart and make him a likely candidate for the kingdom?

Nebuchadnezzar approached the door of the fiery furnace and called the three men to come out. And when they came out, "the satraps, administrators, governors, and the king's counselors gathered together, and they saw these men on whose bodies the fire had no power; the hair of their head was not singed nor were their garments affected, and the smell of fire was not on them" (verse 27).

Oh, Nebuchadnezzar was moved all right. The others must have been amazed and dumbfounded as well. But it was Nebuchadnezzar who voiced what they all felt. "Praise to the God of Shadrach, Meshach and Abednego! He sent his angel to rescue his servants who trusted in him. They defied the king's command and were willing to die rather than serve or worship any god except their own God!" (verse 28, NLT). But then, as we already saw, he added the decree that "if any people, whatever their race or nation or language, speak a word against the God of Shadrach, Meshach, and Abednego, they will be torn limb from limb, and their houses will be crushed into heaps of rubble" (verse 29, NLT).

Because of the overpowering force of God's intervention, Nebuchadnezzar put on record throughout his entire realm that the God of the Hebrews was the only God worthy of supreme adoration. And God was pleased with his confession of faith. However, prideful king that he still was, he overstepped his authority by far in forcing his subjects to make the same confession that he had made. I'm sure God wasn't pleased with that because He doesn't force anyone to worship Him. Instead, He seeks the worship of those who offer it by their own loving free will.

The strongest overture yet

It was still later in his reign, when the memory of the four in the furnace had faded, that Nebuchadnezzar had his most powerful, life-changing encounter with the God of heaven. It started with another dream and another interpretation by Daniel.

This dream warned of such dire consequences for Nebuchadnezzar that Daniel could hardly bring himself to relate it until the king pressed him to do so. Nebuchadnezzar was to be cut down to size. Humbled. His kingdom was to be ripped from his hands for seven years. He would act like a madman and live like an animal, eating grass, and consequently, he would be separated from society for those seven years.

This humiliation didn't fall upon him immediately. A year after the dream, while he was walking in his palace and looking out over the city, he was overcome by the grandeur, the immensity, the glory of Babylon—and he knew himself to be the man behind it all! I like the way *The Clear Word Bible* paraphrases Nebuchadnezzar's words: "I looked out over the city and said to myself, 'What a beautiful sight! I'm the one who built this magnificent city! I'm the one who put this nation on its feet and made it into a great empire! It was my intelligence and power that did all this, no one else's. This great Babylon will stand as a monument to me forever.' "[13]

That did it. The dream was fulfilled. The judgment fell. The two-by-four treatment was administered. But, by the end of those seven years of madness, the proud heathen king had become a humble, heaven-bound, kingdom candidate. Then his sanity returned, and he became king again. And the public acknowledgment of and confession of faith in the God of heaven that Nebuchadnezzar made then, rivals any other in the entire Bible.

Peter's confession of faith in Jesus was noteworthy. When Jesus asked the disciples, "Who do you say that I am?" Peter answered, "You are the Christ, the Son of the living God" (Matthew 16:16). But he did this only in the presence of the disciples—a safe place to acknowledge Jesus. And later, he publicly denied Him three times.

Nicodemus and Joseph did go out on a limb by asking the authorities for the body of Jesus so they could give Him a proper burial. But before the Crucifixion, Nicodemus had kept his belief in Jesus secret. And in the upper room, the unbelieving Thomas called Jesus, "My Lord and my God" (John 20:28), and we cite his confession of faith as commendable. But he made this confession in the presence of just the disciples and only after he had actually touched the wounded hands of the resurrected Savior and put his finger into His side.

Contrast these testimonies with that of Nebuchadnezzar. Though he held a position of power and authority and fame as king of an empire, he wasn't ashamed to write a letter to his whole kingdom, proclaiming his faith in God—a letter that began with these words:

I thought it good to declare the signs and wonders that the Most High God has worked for me.

How great are His signs,
And how mighty His wonders!
His kingdom is an everlasting kingdom,
And His dominion is from generation to generation (Dan-
iel 4:2, 3).

And after the story of his humiliation was told, Nebuchadnezzar gave this testimony: "Now I, Nebuchadnezzar, praise and extol and honor the King of heaven, all of whose works are truth, and His ways justice. And those who walk in pride He is able to put down" (verse 37). This is called a confession of faith. And it comes from a most unlikely candidate for the kingdom, but one who came to see God for who He really is.

I know it isn't scriptural. It's only my imagination. But I can see Nebuchadnezzar and Daniel singing a duet for a worship service in heaven. They're standing close together with their arms on each other's shoulders. Their faces are radiating the very glory of God, and they have resplendent crowns on their heads. Daniel is singing first tenor, and Nebuchadnezzar is singing second.

---

1. White, *Prophets and Kings*, 515.
2. *The Seventh-day Adventist Bible Commentary*, 4:772.
3. Ibid.
4. *The Seventh-day Adventist Bible Commentary*, 4:751.
5. White, *Prophets and Kings*, 515.
6. Pritchard, ed., *Ancient Near Eastern Texts*, 307.
7. White, *Prophets and Kings*, 503, 504.
8. *The Seventh-day Adventist Bible Commentary*, 4:772.
9. Blanco, *The Clear Word Bible*, 962.
10. White, *Prophets and Kings*, 504.
11. Ibid.
12. *The Seventh-day Adventist Bible Commentary*, 4:758.
13. Blanco, *The Clear Word Bible*, 962 (Daniel 4:30).

Questions for Reflection and Discussion

1. Does God have favorites? If so, was Nebuchadnezzar one of them? Explain.

2. Does God put forth more effort to save some people than others? Explain.

3. What do you think of the patience God showed toward a heathen king?

4. What personal help, inspiration, and/or encouragement do you find in this story?

5. How often did Nebuchadnezzar backslide?

6. Why do some people seem to be cut down in their sins while others are given so many chances?

7. Do you think that by the end of his life Nebuchadnezzar was a professing child of God or was he something else?

Chapter 13
The Woman at the Well

"He [Jesus] needed to go through Samaria" (John 4:4).

Much of the rest of this chapter of Scripture is devoted to the story of Jesus' encounter with an unnamed woman: "a woman," "the woman." Or, as Jesus addressed her directly one time, "Woman."

Do you find it interesting that some of the unlikelies in the New Testament are nameless? The thief on the cross is. And so is this Samaritan woman. It would almost appear that they are rather insignificant, out there on the fringe of society, just solitary individuals among the nameless masses—except for one thing: the space given in Scripture to telling their stories. And their stories are "the old, old story"[1] of salvation.

Why did Jesus "need" to go through Samaria? Because He knew there was a well there where He could get a drink?

Hardly.

Did He need to go through Samaria because that was the only option He and the disciples had if they wanted to get from where they were to their destination of Galilee?

No. The most direct route went through Samaria, but there were two other routes they could have taken—routes the Jews preferred because they avoided Samaria and the Samaritans.

Or did Jesus go through Samaria in order to meet "the woman" and to reap the harvest from the two-day evangelistic campaign in Sychar that resulted from that meeting?

Knowing the Savior, knowing His deep love for humankind, and knowing that because He was both divine and human and could therefore see into the future and see into hearts in ways that we can't, we have to believe that His meeting the woman at the well was intentional. Jesus didn't stumble into coincidences and just-happened-tos. Nothing that involved the Savior, His presence, and His purpose was just happenstance. Thirty-three years is a relatively short lifetime, and three and one-half years of ministry is even shorter. Jesus was a God-man on a mission. The goal of His laserlike love mission was to save the whole world, which included this one lost sheep at the well. But we're getting ahead of our story.

"So He came to a city of Samaria which is called Sychar, near the plot of ground that Jacob gave to his son Joseph. [Joseph had said he wanted his bones to be buried there.] Now Jacob's well was there. Jesus therefore, being wearied from His journey, sat thus by the well. It was about the sixth hour [approximately noon]. A woman of Samaria came to draw water" (verses 5–7).

Sychar probably is "the modern 'Askar." This may pinpoint the modern-day site of Sychar because of its proximity to Jacob's well, where Jesus rested. "This well is situated about ten minutes' walk below the village of 'Askar, on the road to Jerusalem. No site connected with the life of Jesus is more certainly identified than this well, which still provides water for a monastery garden at the foot of Mt. Gerizim."[2]

So we have the setting and the two protagonists in the story. And now a long list of unlikelies begins.

The list

First, it was unlikely that Jesus could minister to anyone in Samaria. In both blood and religion, the Samaritans were considered to be mongrel Jews. After the captivity of the ten tribes, the king of Assyria planted colonies of pagans in the area that became Samaria. The Samaritans were the product of the intermarriage of these pagans with the poor Jewish people who had been left behind when first Israel and then Judah were overthrown and the higher classes were either killed or deported.

The Samaritans worshiped only one God, the God of Israel, to whom they erected a temple on Mount Gerizim—in competition with the temple in Jerusalem. The Samaritans and Jews despised each other and showed it by their actions. For instance, Luke tells us that the Samaritans wouldn't "receive" Jesus when they saw He was going to Jerusalem (Luke 9:53), and the Jews thought there was no worse put-down than to call someone a Samaritan. When the Jews were prospering, the Samaritans claimed to be their kindred (see Ezra 4:2), but when the Jews were in distress, the Samaritans called themselves Medes and Persians.[3]

The commentator Matthew Henry says the Jews were extremely malicious towards the Samaritans. They " 'looked upon them as having no part in the resurrection, excommunicated and cursed them by the sacred name of God, by the glorious writing of the tables, and by the curse of the upper and lower house of judgment, with this law, That no Israelite eat of any thing that is a Samaritan's, for it is as if he should eat swine's flesh.' "[4] And Ellen White has noted that "a Jew would not borrow from a Samaritan, nor receive a kindness, not even a morsel of bread or a cup of water."[5] So, Samaria wasn't a great location in which to scatter gospel seed. The unlikeliness was palpable.

Second, noon was an unlikely time of day for Jesus to find a woman at the well. Morning and evening were the times when women came to draw water, not in the heat of the day. Morning and evening were the times when a person could find other people there—people who would be willing to talk. Noon was the wrong time of day for that. But maybe this woman wanted it that way. Maybe because of her lifestyle, she was more comfortable coming to the well when no one else was there.

Third, it was extremely unlikely that Jesus and this Samaritan would have a conversation. It was unlikely that a man would talk to a woman who wasn't a relative—especially in these circumstances. Out there by the well? No one else around? What might people think? "Among the Jews it was considered highly improper for a man, and beneath the dignity of a rabbi, to converse with a woman in public. An ancient Jewish literary work . . . advises, 'Let no one talk with a woman in the street, no, not with his own wife.' "[6] We know what the disciples thought when they returned from buying food in Sychar and found Jesus talking to her. They *"marveled* that He talked with a woman" (John 4:27; emphasis added). That's what they thought! And the unlikeliness was doubled by the fact that the woman was a Samaritan.

Scripture says that when the disciples came, none of them asked, " 'What do You seek?' or, 'Why are You talking with her?' " (verse 27). No. They were too much a part of the culture of that day to probe Jesus' actions. Perhaps they also had too much respect for their Master to put Him on the spot. But a woman? A *poor* woman? A stranger? And a Samaritan? The disciples had to exchange quick questioning glances. They had to be thinking,

What's this about? We've never seen Him do anything like this before. He's always been more reserved than this!

The woman herself was greatly perplexed by the incident too. "Then the woman of Samaria said to Him, 'How is it that You, being a Jew, ask a drink from me, a Samaritan woman?' " (verse 9). Jesus was breaking down cultural and racial barriers. He was disregarding them because He wanted nothing to stand in the way of His offer.

What Jesus offered

What was Jesus offering the woman? He said, "If you knew . . . who it is who says to you, 'Give Me a drink,' you would have asked Him, and He would have given you living water" (verse 10). He was offering her never-thirst-again, living water.

The Samaritan woman totally misunderstood Jesus' offer. She didn't get it. All she could think of was never again having to go through the tiring process—the walk to the well in the heat of the day, lowering the water vessel on a long rope, pulling it and its heavy load of water back up, and then carrying the water back home. Of course, Nicodemus—a male and a religious leader—didn't get Jesus' point either when Jesus told Nicodemus he must be born again, so we mustn't fault the Samaritan woman too heavily.

The Savior immediately turned the conversation towards deeply personal matters. He told the woman, "Go, call your husband, and come here" (verse 16).

The woman replied, "I have no husband" (verse 17). In a sense, she was correct, because although she had been married five times, she was now living with a man whom she hadn't married. Her misleading response shows she didn't know who she was talking to. Certainly, she had no idea where her response would lead.

The Divine Physician had to cut before He could heal. He had to wound before He could make well. "You have well said, 'I have no husband,' " He commented, "for you have had five husbands, and the one whom you now have is not your husband" (verses 17, 18).

Maybe the woman had thought that if she said, "I have no husband," Jesus would conclude that she was single or that she was a widow. Of course, she was neither. At this point, she was living with another man. And somehow, we can't believe that she had lost all five former husbands in death, so very likely she was living in an adulterous relationship, in open sin.

In a sense, her response to Jesus' revealing portrait of her life was an un-likely one—this time, in a positive way. She could have said, "This conversation is over." She could have just turned her back and walked away. Instead, rather surprisingly, her reaction wasn't one of anger or castigation or self-defense. Rather, she said respectfully, "Sir, I perceive that You are a prophet" (verse 19).

However, a defense mechanism did surface too. This conversation was getting too close to home. Too personal. The woman parried Jesus' thrust by changing the subject. She brought up the perennial argument between the Jews and the Samaritans about where one should worship—on Mount Gerizim or in Jerusalem. Anything to turn the conversation away from her own secrets, her personal life, past and present.

However, "Jesus had convinced her that He read the secrets of her life; yet she felt that He was her friend, pitying and loving her. While the very purity of His presence condemned her sin, He had spoken no word of denunciation, but had told her of His grace, that could renew the soul."[7]

Her unlikely response was, " 'I know that Messiah is coming' (who is called Christ). 'When He comes, He will tell us all things' " (verse 25).

Then Jesus did another unlikely thing. He told this Samaritan woman, "I who speak to you am He" (verse 26).

Jesus didn't make this planet-shaking revelation to the crowds. He certainly didn't make it to the religious officials. He made it to an unlikely person of unlikely gender and unlikely race.

The woman's response

The disciples returned at this point, and the one-on-one dynamic was over—but not the change the woman had begun to experience because of the profound impact of Jesus' visit with her. John 4:28 says, "The woman then left her waterpot, [and] went her way into the city." Did she leave the waterpot so the men could have a drink? Was she so excited about her recent conversation that she forgot her original mission? Was she uncomfortable in the presence of all those Jewish men?

More than likely she was excited and focused. She had just met the Messiah. She had looked upon Him, talked with Him. Forget the water! Forget the pot! Forget that her whole sordid life had been unmasked! Forget everything! This singular, amazing encounter was a once-in-a-lifetime kind of thing, and it was consuming her. She was amazed. She was dazed. She was dumbfounded. It was all she could think about!

And then she bore an unlikely witness. She spilled out her wonder and amazement to "the men" (verse 28). Despite the cultural and religious proscriptions she was breaking, she couldn't keep from telling what had happened to her. And something *had* happened to her. An epiphany? A revelation? A singular manifestation of a Divine Being? All of the above—and more!

Max Lucado pictures Jesus' revelation and her response like this:

> Remarkable. . . . It wasn't within the colonnades of a Roman court that he [Jesus] announced his identity.
>
> No, it was in the shade of a well in a rejected land to an ostracized woman. His eyes must have danced as he whispered the secret.
>
> "I am the Messiah.". . .
>
> Don't miss the drama of the moment. Look at her eyes, wide with amazement. Listen to her as she struggles for words. "Y-y-y-you a-a-a-are the M-m-m-messiah!". . .
>
> Suddenly the insignificance of her life was swallowed by the significance of the moment. "God is here! God has come! God cares . . . for me!". . .
>
> That is why she grabbed the first person she saw and announced her discovery, "I just talked to a man who knows everything I ever did . . . and he loves me anyway!"[8]

How important for us all to remember that when the Samaritan woman saw who Christ was, when she believed that He was the Messiah, the Deliverer, the long-hoped-for One, the One who would make a difference for Israel and Israelites, and when her faith reached out and embraced who He was and what He could do, she immediately acted on her belief. She had some knowledge of religion because she knew about the Messiah coming. She knew that a place of worship was important, and she believed that Mount Gerizim was that place. But all of this was head knowledge. Her conversation with Jesus made religion a personal thing. Now it was a matter of the heart. She had seen and heard for herself, and she was moved. She was compelled. Knowledge and faith had melded into an experiential something, and she felt white-hot motivation.

We don't know about her theology or her grasp of all of the fundamentals of faith. It seems probable she didn't have much of either. But that really wasn't the most important factor. She was now a witness. She had a testimony. Something to say. Something to tell. And no matter how simple it was, it was hers. "He told me all that I ever did." The Scripture records her testimony two times.

Her witness contained two other parts as well. After she told what she had experienced, she gave an invitation: "Come, see a Man . . ." (verse 29)—an approach that Jesus Himself used again and again, "Come." She didn't have to memorize anything. She didn't have to attend a seminar on personal witnessing. It just came out. She couldn't help herself. "Come."

The second part was a question: "Could this be the Christ?" (verse 29). That question was both provocative and compelling.

Because the men who heard her testimony could see the conviction in her face and hear it in her voice, "they went out of the city and came to Him" (verse 30). And more than this, "many of the Samaritans of that city believed in Him *because of the word of the woman who testified, 'He told me all that I ever did' "* (verse 39; emphasis added).

And there's still more! "So when the Samaritans had come to Him, they urged Him to stay with them [Samaritans asking a Jew to stay with them!]; and He stayed there two days. And *many more* believed because of His own word" (verses 40, 41; emphasis added).

What did they believe?

"This is indeed the Christ, the Savior of the world" (verse 42).

Breathtaking!

And it wouldn't have been surprising if many people flocked to someone to have their fortune told or their past revealed, but these came to One who would tell them of their faults, their sins, and their duty. Ah, but He also offered them hope and the water of life everlasting.

A one-sentence testimony from "that kind of a woman," and a two-day evangelistic reaping meeting by a Jewish Rabbi in hostile territory, and look what happened!

Will she be in the kingdom?

Did she change? Did the conviction she felt make any difference in her life? Did that short experience with Jesus constitute a temporary high of emotions that lasted for a few fleeting moments or days or weeks, or was it something real, something lasting—maybe a forever something? Did the woman go on as before, returning to her "live-in" as though she had never met Jesus? Did she make a trip to Jerusalem so that by the next Sabbath she could worship in the right temple?

We don't know the particulars, but we have to consider the pieces of evidence that strongly suggest she had a conversion experience and will be in the coming kingdom. As one commentator has said, "There is seldom an instance of so remarkable success as this."[9] From a single conversation, in an unlikely place and in unlikely circumstances and with the help of a person of questionable morals, many sinners were converted and many more came to hear the Man the woman spoke of and eventually believed because they themselves heard Him.

Of this woman, Ellen White wrote,

> The woman had been filled with joy as she listened to Christ's words. The wonderful revelation was almost overpowering. . . . With heart overflowing with gladness, she hastened on her way, to impart to others the precious light she had received.
>
> . . . Her words touched their hearts [the hearts of the men of Sychar]. There was a new expression on her face, a change in her whole appearance.[10]

> As soon as she had *found the Saviour* the Samaritan woman brought others to Him. . . . Through the woman whom they despised, a whole cityful were brought to hear the Saviour. She carried the light at once to her countrymen.
>
> This woman represents the working of a *practical faith in Christ*. Every true disciple is born into the kingdom of God as a missionary. He who drinks of the living water becomes a fountain of life. The receiver becomes a giver. The grace of Christ in the soul is like a spring in the desert, welling up to refresh all, and making those who are ready to perish eager to drink of the water of life.[11]

From every human point of view, the woman at the well was an unlikely candidate for the kingdom. But all the evidence suggests she will be blessed *with* the kingdom and *in* the kingdom.

Now, were you thinking that you are an unlikely candidate for the kingdom?

---

1. Katherine Hankey, "Tell Me the Old, Old Story," in *The Seventh-day Adventist Hymnal*, no. 196.

2. *The Seventh-day Adventist Bible Commentary*, 5:937; emphasis in original.

3. See Josephus, *Antiquities of the Jews*, 11.340, 341; 12.257, referenced in Matthew Henry, "John IV," in *Matthew to John*, vol. 5 of *Commentary on the Whole Bible* (Grand Rapids, Mich.: Christian Classics Ethereal Library, 2000), http://www.ccel.org/ccel/henry/mhc5.John.v.html.

4. Dr. Lightfoot, quoted in Matthew Henry, "John IV," in *Matthew to John*, vol. 5 of *Commentary on the Whole Bible* (Grand Rapids, Mich.: Christian Classics Ethereal Library, 2000), http://www.ccel.org/ccel/henry/mhc5.John.v.html.

5. White, *The Desire of Ages*, 183.

6. *The Seventh-day Adventist Bible Commentary*, 5:941.

7. White, *The Desire of Ages*, 189.

8. Max Lucado, *Six Hours One Friday* (Sisters, Ore.: Multnomah Books, 1989), quoted in *The Inspirational Study Bible*, NCV, ed. Max Lucado (Dallas: Word Publishing, 1995), 1261.

9. Albert Barnes, *Barnes' Notes on the New Testament*, ed. Ingram Cobbin (Grand Rapids, Mich.: Kregel Publications, 1962), 285.

10. White, *The Desire of Ages*, 191.

11. Ibid., 195; emphasis added.

Questions for Reflection and Discussion

1. Why did Jesus breach the culture of His day so often? How much attention should we pay to the culture of the society in which we live? How much attention should we pay to the culture of the people we're trying to bring to Jesus?

2. Do you use words such as *luck, happenstance,* and *accidentally* to describe unusual spiritual interactions that you have with people? Is God behind all of our interactions with other people? Explain.

3. Discuss the wisdom of Jesus' opening words to the woman, "Give Me a drink" (John 4:7).

4. Are you uncomfortable with Jesus' words to the woman, "Go, call your husband, and come here"? Were His words too direct? Prying? Offensive? Would you have used those words? What limits should we observe when we're witnessing?

5. How much knowledge must someone have to be saved?

6. Why did the words of a woman with a bad reputation have such a powerful effect on those to whom she witnessed? Do people who are converted after they have lived immoral, evil lives make better witnesses or evangelists than people who have served God all of their lives?

7. What part of the story of the woman at the well hits you hardest?

Chapter 14

From Thief to Saint in
Twenty-two Words

"Lord, remember me when You come into Your kingdom." . . .

"Assuredly, I say to you . . . today[,] you will be with Me in Paradise"
(Luke 23:42, 43).*

Twenty-two words!

You mean it took only about ten seconds for someone to pass from damnation to salvation? A sinner became a saint that fast? On his way to hell,
and then, in ten seconds, on his way to heaven? Incredible!

Yes, the story of the thief is this simple and this fast.

He saw himself.

He saw Jesus.

He turned to Jesus and asked Him if he could be in heaven with Him.

And Jesus said, "Yes."

Thief.† (What a moniker! And how unfortunate that this is the tagline for
one of God's children who will assuredly stand near God's throne—kind of
like "the harlot Rahab," whose name is always accompanied with that unsavory description. These two people have been stigmatized throughout
the ages.)

Scripture doesn't give us this man's name. It's true that in the apoc-
ryphal Gospel of Nicodemus the two thieves crucified with Jesus are
given the names of Dysmas and Gysmas (or Dismas and Gestas). It's
also true that these two names still appear in certain Calvaries and sta-
tions of the cross in some Roman Catholic lands, but this is a matter of

---

*I've modified the punctuation in this quotation to make it consistent with the
biblical teaching on life after death (see later in this chapter).

†See the King James Version of Matthew 27:38 and Mark 15:27.

tradition rather than of Scripture, so we can give these names little if any credence.

His unlikely background

Scripture contains few details about this thief (let's call him Dismas), but there are some things we know for sure. Our introduction to him comes at the worst possible time of his life, and the worst possible time in the lives of the two crucified with him—another thief on the other side, and the One in the middle, who was placed there to indicate that He was the worst of the three.

In several translations, Luke 23:39 calls him simply a "criminal." The King James Version uses the word *malefactor*—in other words, *evildoer* or *wrongdoer*. Mark 15 uses different terms for this unlikely candidate for the kingdom: "robber" (NKJV) and "bandit" (NRSV) in verse 27, and "transgressor" (NKJV) and "lawless" (NRSV, margin) in verse 28. None of these terms are flattering, but Luke 23:41 says that Dismas admitted his guilt and was sentenced to the worst possible type of execution for his crimes.

Finally, Matthew 27:44 also gives us a snapshot of Dismas's unlikelihood. The chief priests, scribes, and elders had just taunted Jesus: "He saved others; Himself He cannot save. If He is the King of Israel, let Him now come down from the cross, and we will believe Him. He trusted in God; let Him deliver Him now if He will have Him; for He said, 'I am the Son of God' " (verses 42, 43). Then follows this damning sentence: "Even the *robbers who were crucified with Him reviled Him* with the same thing" (emphasis added). Apparently, both thieves echoed the malevolent words of the Jewish leaders. They both said "the same thing" to Christ. This shows Dismas's hard-heartedness and his unrepentant attitude in the first hours he was on the cross, definitely putting him in the "unlikely" category. He wasn't thinking about the kingdom at that point. Certainly, he wasn't ready yet to ask, "Remember me."

Even Dismas's last-minute request, "Remember me," could easily cast him in the "unlikely" category. Were his motives pure? After all, if you were about to drown, wouldn't you grab the nearest straw, hoping it would save you? With only hours to live, why not get on the kingdom bandwagon? And let's not forget that Dismas didn't even have a chance to prove himself, to demonstrate his sincerity, to show his change of heart. So, what about sanctification and overcoming? He didn't have time for any of that, so how do we know that his conversion was real?

Some people find it difficult to believe that anyone could make such a sudden change and be accepted by the Savior. They think of our man as kind of a "Christian thief." Perhaps they consider him to be a lapsed Christian or a backslidden Christian—someone who, at one point, had all of his theological ducks in a row only to knock them out of line—but who returned to faith when he was facing imminent death.

There is little, if any, evidence to support this supposition. The beautiful commentary on the life of Christ, *The Desire of Ages,* says this man "was not a hardened criminal." That's good. However, the same book tells us that Dismas "had seen and heard Jesus, and had been convicted by His teaching, but he had been turned away from Him by the priests and rulers," and then he had "plunged deeper and deeper into sin."[1] It seems that we must let him be what he was. A "malefactor." A robber—a criminal—a transgressor who deserved to die for his crimes. Condemned by human judgment, and a sinner in God's eyes.

But right next to him on the cross, at that very moment, in the torture of his final hours, was the Man in the middle about whom it was written "This Man receives sinners" (Luke 15:2); "God demonstrates His own love toward us, in that while we were still sinners, Christ died for us" (Romans 5:8); and "This is a faithful saying and worthy of all acceptance, that Christ Jesus came into the world to save sinners" (1 Timothy 1:15). So whatever Dismas was called—malefactor, thief, criminal, robber, transgressor— salvation was only an earshot away! Unlikely candidate for the kingdom or likely candidate for the kingdom—the difference was only a few feet away. Only a choice away.

Dismas's coming to faith

Something happened to Dismas in a matter of a few hours. Remember, at first he had reviled Jesus. He had spoken doubting, mocking, blasphemous words against Him. At that point, he was joining the priests, scribes, elders, and the other thief in taunting Jesus. He thought the same thing. He said the same thing. But a short time later, he turned to Jesus and said, "Lord, remember me when You come into Your kingdom." What was this about? Why the sudden turnaround? What happened in his mind? Why the change of heart?

The biblical record is sketchier than we would wish, but there are some informative implications. First, Dismas had been listening to what the people were saying about Jesus. He heard the words of faith and mourning from believers as well as the words full of unbelief and hatred from the unfeeling synagogue officials and the curious rabble.

More than that, he had seen and heard Jesus' reactions—what He said and how He said it. He had heard Jesus say, "Father, forgive them, for they do not know what they do" (Luke 23:34). Maybe hearing those words was enough. Such meekness! Such pity! Such love! Such forbearance! A response so void of retaliation and revenge. Dismas had never seen or heard anything like this in his life. What kind of a Man was this?

Ellen White pictures the change in these words:

> There is no question now. There are no doubts, no reproaches. When condemned for his crime, the thief had become hopeless and despairing; but strange, tender thoughts now spring up. He calls to mind all he has heard of Jesus, how He has healed the sick and pardoned sin. He has heard the words of those who believed in Jesus and followed Him weeping. He has seen and read the title above the Saviour's head. He has heard the passers-by repeat it, some with grieved, quivering lips, others with jesting and mockery. The Holy Spirit illuminates his mind, and little by little the chain of evidence is joined together.[2]

This surely must have been Dismas's thinking, for when the other thief said, "If You are the Christ, save Yourself and us" (verse 39), Dismas turned to him and said, " 'Dost not thou fear God, seeing thou art in the same condemnation?' The dying thieves have no longer anything to fear from man. But upon one of them presses the conviction that there is a God to fear, a future to cause him to tremble. And now, all sin-polluted as it is, his life history is about to close. 'And we indeed justly,' he moans; 'for we receive the due reward of our deeds: but this Man hath done nothing amiss.' "[3]

Yes, it must have been this way. "In Jesus, bruised, mocked, and hanging upon the cross, he sees the Lamb of God, that taketh away the sin of the world. Hope is mingled with anguish in his voice as the helpless, dying soul casts himself upon a dying Saviour. 'Lord, remember me,' he cries, 'when Thou comest into Thy kingdom.' "[4]

One thief wanted to be saved from the cross. The other wanted to be saved from sin. These mind-sets are as far apart as heaven and hell.

The kingdom? Unquestionably

Can you imagine the difference a day makes?

> Twelve hours before, this man was a hardened criminal, habitu-ated to a life of rapacious and murderous violence; his counterpart is to be found to-day in the cells of a penal establishment. And now, after a short companionship with Jesus, after hearing him speak and seeing him suffer, his heart is purged and cleansed of its iniquity, he is another man, he is a child of God, an heir of heaven. There are great capacities in these human souls of ours, which do not come often into exercise, but which are actually within us. Powerful speech, imminent peril, great emergencies, sudden inspiration from God,—these and other things will call them forth; there is a brilliant flash of remembrance, or of emotion, or of realization, or of conviction and resolution. And then that which is ordinarily wrought in many days or months is accomplished in an hour. The movements of our mind are not subject to any time-table calcula-tions whatsoever. No man can define the limit of possibility here. Great revolutions can be and have been wrought almost momen-tarily. Not slowly toiling upward step by step, but more swiftly than the uprising of the strongest bird upon fleetest wing, may the human soul ascend from the darkness of death into the radiant sunshine of hope and life.[5]

There's no question whether this unlikely candidate will be in the king-dom. The promise of the Kingdom-Giver Himself is beautifully pictured in these words: "Quickly the answer came. Soft and melodious the tone, full of love, compassion, and power the words: Verily I say unto thee today, Thou shalt be with Me in Paradise."[6]

Think of it! In a twenty-two word conversation, a perhaps ten-second ex-change, Dismas went from wrong to redeemed. From a perfect mess to a perfect man. From lawbreaker to law keeper. From son of the devil to son of the living God. From total wickedness to total righteousness. From sinner to saint. From hell and eternal damnation to heaven and eternal salvation.

There are those who believe that Jesus promised Dismas that he would be with Him in Paradise—heaven—that very day. John 20:17 shows that He couldn't have made—or fulfilled—that promise because He was crucified on Friday, and on the following Sunday He told Mary, "I have not yet ascended to My Father." No, Jesus was promising that when He returns to earth to take home those who have received Him, Dismas will most assuredly be among them.* One Bible commentary expresses it succinctly: "The great question the thief was pondering at the moment was not *when* he would reach paradise, but whether he would get there at all."[7]

As is true of most commentaries, the author of *The Desire of Ages* has no question about Dismas's salvation: "None acknowledged Him as He hung dying upon the cross save the penitent thief *who was saved at the eleventh hour.*"[8] "To the penitent thief came the perfect peace *of acceptance with God.*"[9] Praise God from whom all *salvation* flows!

In His sermon on the mount, Jesus said, "Be perfect" (Matthew 5:48). Did Dismas reach this exalted state in the blink of an eye? Is it possible that an unlikely, unspiritual, imperfect, lost, dying criminal can experience character perfection—meet heaven's entrance requirements—in a few hours? Was he a perfect anything other than a perfect thief? How does one go from being a perfect flop to being just plain perfect in the last few hours of life?

Note what Ellen White wrote about moral perfection and salvation: "Angelic perfection failed in heaven. Human perfection failed in Eden, the paradise of bliss. *All who wish for security in earth or heaven must look to the Lamb of God.*"[10]

Lest anyone take license from this story of the thief, I offer this caution: Don't count on waiting to the last minute to repent, to reach for the straw, to grab the lifeline. The Lord might see through that! All should remember the words expressed by Matthew Henry: "This gives no encouragement to any to put off their repentance to their death-bed, or to hope that then they shall find mercy; for, though it is certain that true repentance is never too late, it is as certain that late repentance is seldom true."[11]

Conversely, be encouraged that extreme unlikeliness and extreme salvation aren't really that far apart. Dismas proved that!

---

*The original writers of the books of the Bible didn't use punctuation. It was added centuries later—not always correctly.

1. White, *The Desire of Ages,* 749.

2. Ibid., 750.

3. Ibid.

4. Ibid.

5. W. Clarkson, "Homilies by Various Authors [on the Book of Luke 23:39–43]," in *Mark & Luke,* vol. 16 of *The Pulpit Commentary,* eds. H. D. M. Spence and Joseph S. Exell (Grand Rapids, Mich.: Eerdmans, 1950), 258 (see homily on Luke 23:39–43).

6. White, *The Desire of Ages,* 750.

7. *The Seventh-day Adventist Bible Commentary,* 5:878; emphasis in original.

8. White, *The Desire of Ages,* 751; emphasis added.

9. Ibid.; emphasis added.

10. Ellen G. White, *Our High Calling* (Washington, D.C.: Review and Herald®, 1961), 45; emphasis added.

11. Matthew Henry, "Luke XXIII," in *Matthew to John,* vol. 5 of *Commentary on the Whole Bible* (Grand Rapids, Mich.: Christian Classics Ethereal Library, 2000), http://www.ccel.org/ccel/henry/mhc5.Luke.xxiv.html.

Questions for Reflection and Discussion

1. Which of the following sentences best describe your reaction to the thief's obtaining last-minute salvation?
   a. It was too easy.
   b. It wasn't fair.
   c. It was wonderful.
   d. It's a reason to be thankful.
   e. It was an example of amazing grace.
   f. It encourages me.

2. Do the assertions "it's hard to be lost," and "it's easy to be saved" mean the same thing? Explain. Which is closer to the truth? Which do you prefer? Why?

3. What's your reaction to the statement "salvation is beautifully simple and simply beautiful"?

4. Would you say the thief was saved? Explain.

5. Would you use the word *saved* to describe your spiritual state at this moment?

6. Is Paul more deserving of heaven than the thief? Explain.

7. What does the story of the thief tell us about God? About sanctification? About the idea that the Christian life is "a battle and a march"? About works?

Chapter 15
Jovan the Jailer

The incident began when a slave girl "with a spirit of divination" annoyed the apostle Paul (Acts 16:16; see also verse 18). He commanded the spirit, in the name of Christ, to come out of the girl. When it did, the sideshow men who had profited from her problem dragged Paul and Silas to the authorities and charged them with teaching unlawful customs.

The judges went along with the mob, had Paul and Silas's clothes ripped off and ordered a public beating. After beating them black and blue, they threw them into jail, telling the jailkeeper to put them under heavy guard so there would be no chance of escape. He did just that—threw them into the maximum security cell in the jail and clamped leg irons on them.

Along about midnight, Paul and Silas were at prayer and singing a robust hymn to God. The other prisoners couldn't believe their ears. Then, without warning, a huge earthquake! The jailhouse tottered, every door flew open, all the prisoners were loose.

Startled from sleep, the jailer saw all the doors swinging loose on their hinges. Assuming that all the prisoners had escaped, he pulled out his sword and was about to do himself in, figuring he was as good as dead anyway, when Paul stopped him: "Don't do that! We're all still here! Nobody's run away!"

The jailer got a torch and ran inside. Badly shaken, he collapsed in front of Paul and Silas. He led them out of the jail and asked, "Sirs, what do I have to do to be saved, to really live?" They said, "Put your entire trust in the Master Jesus. Then you'll live as you were meant to live—and everyone in your house included!"

They went on to spell out in detail the story of the Master—the entire family got in on this part. They never did get to bed that night. The jailer made them feel at home, dressed their wounds, and then—he couldn't wait till morning!—was baptized, he and everyone in his family. There in his home, he had food set out for a festive meal. It was a night to remember: He and his entire family had put their trust in God; everyone in the house was in on the celebration (Acts 16:22–34, *The Message*).

Once again, the story of an unlikely is told but the unlikely's name isn't given. Once again, as in the cases of the Samaritan woman and of the thief, we have a nameless nobody. These three have something else in common besides being nameless in Scripture. Their reputations. The three nameless ones are a loose woman, a thief, and an unsavory Roman jailer.

Could it be that the names of these three unlikelies were left unrecorded by divine design? They were near the bottom of the social totem pole, and they certainly weren't at the top of the list of likely candidates for the kingdom of God. Is it possible that our God, who is so full of love and compassion and grace, wanted us to grasp just how far down He reaches—that He reaches to the most unworthy, the most unlikely, the most "unsaveable" people on planet Earth so they can be lifted up, utterly transformed, and placed with "the pure and the blest" in God's presence, in God's kingdom, for all of eternity? If so, that would be downright encouraging for the likes of us!

However, for this chapter, let's give the jailer a first-century Roman name. Let's call him Jovan. Jovan the jailer.

An unlikely story

The story of Jovan the jailer has to rank as almost equal with that of the thief on the cross in its unlikelihood. The dungeon prison, the earthquake, the near suicide, the lightning-quick conversion, the salvation of his whole family and household—who could have dreamt up this scenario? Would you start a gospel story with the preachers in jail for corrupting the morals of the populace? If you were looking for fertile ground in which to sow the gospel seed, would a jailer, a warden, a prison-system official come to mind? Would you single out as your prime candidate for salvation and the kingdom a heathen soldier who most likely swore allegiance to Caesar as his god?

The story is so brief and sketchy that it raises a lot of interesting questions.

- Paul and Silas stayed to help the jailer. Why didn't the other prisoners escape? Did they realize that a miracle was taking place?
- What is the chance of the chains of every prisoner falling off at the same time?
- Were the other prisoners close enough to Paul and Silas to hear their prayers and hymn singing?
- Were any of those other prisoners converted, their lives changed, kingdom bound?
- What made Jovan fall down trembling before Paul and Silas?
- Where did Jovan the jailer's question "What must I do to be saved?" come from (verse 30)? What did he know about "being saved"?
- How long was it from earthquake to baptism? Are we looking at a gospel outreach, evangelistic series, and baptismal preparation class all taking place in two or three hours?
- Did Jovan and his family become charter members of the First Philippian Church?
- Might he have been elected as head elder there?

Enough speculation—it's interesting, but secondary. Jovan's story is what we want to look at, and God has chosen to reveal only those portions of his experience that are of the highest importance and have the greatest impact.

"What a scene! The dark inner dungeon; the prisoners fast in the stocks, their backs still bleeding and smarting from the stripes; the companionship of criminals and outcasts of society; the midnight hour; and not groans, or curses, or complaints, but joyous trustful songs of praise ringing through the vault! while their companions in the jail listened with astonishment to the heavenly sound in that place of shame and sorrow."[1]

We don't know whether or not Jovan the jailer actually heard the prayers and hymns of Paul and Silas. It does seem that he was sleeping till the earthquake jarred him awake. But the other prisoners heard the two apostles. "With astonishment the other prisoners heard the sound of prayer and singing issuing from the inner prison. They had been accustomed to hear shrieks and moans, cursing and swearing, breaking the silence of the night; but never before had they heard words of prayer and praise ascending from that gloomy cell. Guards and prisoners marveled and asked themselves who these men could be, who, cold, hungry, and tortured, could yet rejoice."[2]

Without doing damage to the story, we can assume that the jailer might have known something about the two prisoners, Paul and Silas. After all, Acts 16:19–22 says the two were "dragged . . . into the marketplace" (the town square), "then the multitude rose up together against them," the magistrates ripped off their clothes and then commanded them to be beaten, and all of this was done in the open. It's unlikely that the jailer slept through all of that.

The magistrates commanded Jovan "to keep them securely" (verse 23). He took that charge seriously and not only put them in the inner prison (maximum security) but also "fastened their feet in the stocks" (verse 24). Stocks were designed to hold the most dangerous prisoners securely.

And then the earthquake! As someone has written, "No stone of the prison building but it moved, no locked door but it opened, no fetter [shackle] but it was loosed."[3] The building was shaken, and so were the people—particularly the jailer. God doesn't always manifest Himself in a still, small Voice.

The jailer had probably been a Roman soldier, and the command of the town magistrates had been clear and strong. So, when the earthquake opened all the prison doors and loosed the chains from all the prisoners and he thought all of them had escaped, he quickly concluded that the only honorable way out was for him to kill himself. Besides, that way he could avoid all the humiliation and punishment that he would soon suffer. So, it's not difficult to imagine what his feelings were when he heard Paul shout, "Don't hurt yourself. We're all here!" No wonder he called for a light and ran to Paul and Silas's cell and "fell down trembling" before them (verse 29)!

The simplicity of salvation

The real wonder is that the jailer's first words to the apostles were, "Sirs, what must I do to be saved?" (verse 30). Where'd this come from? What did the jailer mean by "saved"? Saved from what? What did he know about salvation?

We're forced to conclude that maybe earthquakes (and foxholes and . . .)

can do this to people—can motivate them to ask questions about personal salvation. They provide teachable moments—salvation moments.

The marvel of Jovan the jailer's story is twofold: simplicity and brevity. Look again. When Jovan asked, "What must I do to be saved?" Paul and Silas said, "Believe on the Lord Jesus Christ, and you will be saved" (verse 31). They didn't say, "Put your all on the altar." They didn't say, "Fall on the Rock and be broken." They didn't even say, "Repent and be baptized," as Peter did on the Day of Pentecost. They just told Jovan, "Believe on the Lord Jesus Christ, and you will be saved." Amazingly simple.

This inspired formula for salvation sounds as simple as what passed between the thief and Jesus as they hung on their crosses: " 'Lord, remember me when You come into Your kingdom.' . . . 'Assuredly, I say to you . . . today[,] you will be with Me in Paradise' " * (Luke 23:42, 43). Is this salvation summarized? Why, it sounds like what Jesus told Nicodemus, "God so loved the world that He gave His only begotten Son, that whoever *believes in Him* should not perish but have everlasting life" (John 3:16; emphasis added). Shall we say "distilled salvation"?

The words of Paul and Silas to Jovan are also strikingly parallel to what Philip said to the Ethiopian eunuch when the eunuch asked Philip if he could be baptized. "Philip said, 'If you *believe* with all your heart [in Jesus as the Son of God], you may' " (Acts 8:37; emphasis added). He did, and he was! Pretty simple.

At the same time, we must be cautious not to leave the impression that to only believe is the end of it for the new Christian, for it is not just "only believe" but also "and keep on believing." It is not only "Come to Christ" but "keep on coming." It is more than a once-and-for-all something; it is a continuing submission to Jesus Christ, to His Word, His law, His will, and His way. It is permitting the Lord Jesus Christ to work "in you both to will and to do for His good pleasure" (Philippians 2:13). It is "He who has begun a good work in you will complete it until the day of Jesus Christ" (Philippians 1:6).

We must not forget, while we are reveling in the beauty and simplicity of salvation, that Acts 16:32 says, "They *spoke the word of the Lord* to him and to all who were in his house" (emphasis added). How much did they share? What did they emphasize about the Old Testament? Did they repeat the

---

*Regarding the altered punctuation in this verse, see the footnote early in chapter 14 and the explanation toward the end of that chapter.

giving of the commandments in Exodus 20? Did they trace the prophecies of Christ as the Messiah? Did their Bible study last an hour? Two? Did they instruct Jovan and his family about Christian lifestyle? We don't know, but we do know that they "spoke the word of the Lord to them," and this followed and amplified the beautiful simplicity of "Believe on the Lord Jesus Christ, and you will be saved."

However much instruction Jovan and his household received, and however much faith these new believers displayed, they followed it up by taking the next steps. They made a decision. They made a commitment. They began to obey. They were baptized. And, praise God, the fruits of faith began to appear in their lives.

Jovan brought Paul and Silas into his house. He washed and cleansed their wounds. He fed them. His newfound faith immediately blossomed into acts of love and kindness. As James said, "Show me your faith without your works, and I will show you my faith *by* my works" (James 2:18; emphasis added). God was already at work in this sincere believer, who immediately demonstrated that he had the faith that works by love (see Galatians 5:6).

What are we looking at? Instantaneous belief. Instantaneous conversion. Instantaneous salvation. Instantaneous works of righteousness. How can we do anything but marvel and praise God? The simplicity of it all; the brevity of it all. From unlikely to likely in a few short hours.

"Thus do the darkest places and most repulsive associations become glorified and idealized by the Spirit of the living and loving God. The prison becomes a chapel; a dread place of judgment; a school of penitence and faith; a home of love and kindness; a place of new birth and new life."[4] As someone succinctly put it, "The jailor [sic] has become a 'prisoner of Jesus Christ.' "[5]

The final biblical scene in which we find Jovan pictured is in Acts 16:34. This is the icing on the salvation cake. "When he had brought them into his house, he set food before them; and *he rejoiced,* having believed in God with all his household" (emphasis added).

What kind of rejoicing? The Greek suggests "jumping for joy, . . . exalt . . . be (exceedingly) glad."[6] That kind of rejoicing!

And what was the rejoicing about? Sins forgiven, a loving Savior, being on their way to heaven. That could make anyone rejoice!

That Philippian jail had never before witnessed anything like this rejoicing. It was a night that Jovan the jailer and his family would never forget!

———————

1. A. C. Hervey, "Exposition [on the Book of the Acts of the Apostles 16:25]," in *Acts & Romans*, vol. 18 of *The Pulpit Commentary*, eds. H. D. M. Spence and Joseph S. Exell (Grand Rapids, Mich.: Eerdmans, 1950), 31 (see exposition on Acts 16:25).

2. Ellen G. White, *The Acts of the Apostles* (Mountain View, Calif.: Pacific Press®, 1911), 214.

3. P. C. Barker, "Homilies by Various Authors [on the Book of Acts 16:16–39]," in *Acts & Romans*, vol. 18 of *The Pulpit Commentary*, 50 (see homily on Acts 16:16–39).

4. E. Johnson, "Homilies by Various Authors [on the Book of Acts 16:19–34]," in *Acts & Romans*, vol. 18 of *The Pulpit Commentary*, 43 (see homily on Acts 16:19–34).

5. Ibid.

6. Strong, *Strong's Exhaustive Concordance*, Greek entry 21.

Questions for Reflection
and Discussion

1. What is most encouraging to you about the jailer's midnight conversion?

2. How did faith and works function in the jailer's conversion?

3. Could the suddenness of the jailer's salvation give him a false hope? Could it give those who read his story a false hope? Could it make someone presume upon the mercy of God—take unwarranted advantage of His grace?

4. Do you see any dichotomy between the words of Jesus in the gospel commission, "teaching them to observe *all things* that I have commanded you" (Matthew 28:20; emphasis added), and the few hours of study that the jailer and his family did with Paul and Silas before their baptism?

5. Will you change anything in your mode of witnessing because of this story? Explain.

6. How does your faith measure up to that of Paul and Silas—a faith that enabled them to sing and praise God while they were in jail for doing God's work? What could you do to help your faith grow stronger?

7. What questions would you like to ask the jailer?

Chapter 16
Twenty-first Century Unlikelies

In Max Lucado's words,

For thousands of years, using his wit and charm, man had tried to be friends with God. And for thousands of years he had let God down more than he had lifted him up. He's done the very thing he promised he'd never do. It was a fiasco. Even the holiest of the heroes sometimes forgot whose side they were on. Some of the scenarios in the Bible look more like the adventures of Sinbad the sailor than stories for vacation Bible school. Remember these characters?

Aaron. Right-hand man to Moses. Witness of the plagues. Member of the "Red Sea Riverbed Expedition." Holy priest of God. But if he was so saintly, what is he doing leading the Israelites in fireside aerobics in front of the golden calf?

The sons of Jacob. The fathers of the tribes of Israel. Great-grandsons of Abraham. Yet, if they were so special, why were they gagging their younger brother and sending him to Egypt?

David. The man after God's own heart. The King's king. The giant-slayer and songwriter. He's also the guy whose glasses got steamy as a result of a bath on a roof. Unfortunately, the water wasn't his, nor was the woman he was watching.

And Samson. Swooning on Delilah's couch, drunk on the wine, perfume, and soft lights. He's thinking, *She's putting on something more comfortable.* She's thinking, *I know I put those shears in here somewhere.*

Adam adorned in fig leaves and stains of forbidden fruit. Moses throwing both a staff and a temper tantrum. King Saul looking into a crystal ball for the will of God. Noah, drunk and naked in his own tent.

These are the chosen ones of God? This is the royal lineage of the King? These are the ones who were to carry out God's mission?

It's easy to see the absurdity.

Why didn't he give up? Why didn't he let the globe spin off its axis?

Even after generations of people had spit in his face, he still loved them. After a nation of chosen ones had stripped him naked and ripped his incarnated flesh, he still died for them. And even today, after billions have chosen to prostitute themselves before the pimps of power, fame, and wealth, he still waits for them.

It *is* inexplicable. It doesn't have a drop of logic nor a thread of rationality.

And yet, it is that very irrationality that gives the gospel its greatest defense. For only God could love like that.[1]

Note that Lucado mentions only two of the names I've written about in this book as unlikelies: Jacob's sons and Samson. In other words, we each found plenty of unlikelies. Unfortunately, we could generate unending lists of them. This is why I often say that every last one of us is a member of the Six-and-a-Half-Billion Club—we're all human. All of this underscores once more the humanness of all of us, plus the fact that the best of us on this planet are—when we're disconnected from God—chips off the old block. We resemble our original parents: the perfect couple in a perfect Garden with a perfect forever ahead of them, who traded it all away and handed all their descendants the "gift" of being unlikely candidates for the kingdom of heaven. And we, here in the twenty-first century, *we are them*! Or, if you prefer, *they are us*! Say it either way you prefer, just so you understand that we're all included.

In this final chapter, I want to distill my thinking, my heart, my beliefs, my convictions, and my understandings and put them all at the service of displaying fully the total irrationality of the love of God and His unexplainable, amazing, incomprehensible, unfathomable, incredible grace toward all of His earthborn, earthbound creatures. I understand that I make myself vulnerable in doing this, but I proceed.

Brother Serattia*

I was a young ministerial intern in my very first pastoral assignment.

---

*A pseudonym.

The senior pastor was a venerable veteran. (He'd been serving as a minister for five whole years!) We pastored three churches in Southern California: Escondido, San Pasqual, and Ramona. The latter was a small church in a little mountain town. Most of my duties were centered there.

I held some evangelistic meetings in Ramona—my very first. One of the women who attended the meetings, Mrs. Serattia, had once lived as a Christian but had grown careless, worldly, and indifferent to the church and things spiritual. However, she was beginning to respond to the Holy Spirit's call for her to return to faith in Christ and church fellowship.

During the meetings, Mrs. Serattia asked me to come to her house, meet her husband, and share some one-on-one Bible studies with her so she could renew her walk with the Lord. I was more than happy to do this, and we set up a regular weekly schedule. I met Mr. Serattia when I came to study the Bible with his wife.

Mr. Serattia was an old-fashioned blacksmith. He was a hard man, a hard worker who had hard muscles and a very gravelly voice. He drank hard, used hard, foul language, and, from all appearances, had a hard, unbelieving heart. He tolerated my coming to visit his wife and to study the Bible with her, listening night after night, week after week, while he sat in his chair in the corner of the living room in a slightly comatose condition. Occasionally, we heard snoring sounds.

I wanted to cultivate Mr. Serattia's friendship if possible, so sometimes I would visit him at his blacksmith shop in town. He would often be working over his fire, iron tongs in hand, shaping the red-hot metal. When he blew his alcohol-laden breath into the flames I thought the whole little shop might go up in flames!

As my studies with Mrs. Serattia continued, Mr. Serattia began to show some signs of wakefulness if not interest or outright attention, though he still didn't join the discussion. By now, Mrs. Serattia had a deepening interest and was beginning to feel convicted that she should renew her fellowship with Christ and the church.

I well remember the night when she voiced her convictions and asked to be rebaptized to seal her newfound faith. Mr. Serattia was awake at that point, and, for the very first time, he interrupted our conversation. His tender remark, "Well, if you're going to baptize her, just hold her down until the bubbles stop coming." Nice.

Shortly after Mrs. Serattia's baptism, I was asked to assist another senior pastor who was serving the church at the Paradise Valley Sanitarium in National City, and so my wife and I moved to the San Diego area and our contact with the Serattias ended.

Several months later, I received a telephone call from the pastor in Escondido. He asked me to visit Mr. Serattia, who was in a San Diego hospital, having a laryngectomy because he had throat cancer. The pastor said he knew that "Brother Serattia" (I didn't know for sure what he meant by that) would be really glad to see me. He didn't elaborate more than that. As soon as I could, I left for the hospital.

I entered the large hospital, found out Mr. Serattia's room number, and made my way down a long corridor. I knew I was close to Mr. Serattia's room when I heard a familiar, raspy voice. Stopping outside the room, I listened. Hard, old Mr. Serattia was talking to his roommate about Christ and the Bible and salvation! I could hardly believe my ears—but it was him. No mistaking that harsh whisper of a voice.

I rounded the corner, entered the room, and saw his face. It was a different face than the one I remembered—a smiling, shining face now. Mr. Serattia had made a choice—for him an unlikely one—that assured him that he was indeed, through Jesus Christ, a candidate for the kingdom. And he had been baptized.

Our paths didn't cross again for quite a while. Meanwhile, I thought about him and prayed for him. Was this all real? Would his decision be lasting? Was he really on his way "home"?

I saw the Serattias again while attending a large General Conference session in San Francisco with thousands of other like-minded believers. When I looked Mr. Serattia in the face, I knew he was on his way. He had a speech device that enabled him to communicate, but he didn't have to say anything to convince me where he was headed. His smiles, the happiness his face revealed, told everyone that he was headed for our eternal home.

That was the last time I saw Brother Serattia. What a great memory! What a great change he had experienced! What a loving God, One who's full of the grace that can soften and change such a hard, unlikely heart!

There's no proof that Brother Serattia will be in the kingdom. But the gift of God in Christ, His unfailing, unconditional love, His promises, and the countless examples of His grace in operation found in the Bible convince me that not only could he be there, but he absolutely *will* be there.

So, are we lowering the standard by believing in this outrageous grace of God?

Are we misrepresenting the requirements for getting into the kingdom?

Are we guilty of dropping the bar—of making it too easy?

Are we making light of the commandments, of obedience, of the keepings, the doings, the supposed tos, the ought tos, the have tos, the musts, the you-better-or-elses?

Let us be reminded

Let's remember that all of us are unlikely candidates for the kingdom. Every son and daughter of Adam and Eve is unlikely. Hear it from God Himself:

- *"All have sinned* and fall short of the glory of God" (Romans 3:23; emphasis added).
- "There is no one who does not sin" (1 Kings 8:46).
- "In Your sight no one living is righteous" (Psalm 143:2).
- "The LORD looks down from heaven upon the children of men, to see if there are any who understand, who seek God. They have all turned aside, they have together become corrupt; *there is none who does good, no, not one*" (Psalm 14:2, 3; emphasis added).

Talk about unlikely—we are it! No one *merits* being in God's presence. No one *deserves* to be saved. Even the 144,000 who are before the throne "without fault" (Revelation 14:5) will not be there because of their own righteousness—righteousness they've developed with blood, sweat, and tears and a high level of abstinence. They'll be there with robes on all right—white robes that remind them of the perfect, sinless, commandment-keeping righteousness of Jesus Christ, *a gift of grace alone*!

I believe that if both Enoch and the thief on the cross will be in heaven,* there has to be some common denominator for getting there. And there is; the grace of God—period!

If Paul will be there and the jailer will be there, then being there—being in God's kingdom—has to be *all of grace*!

---

*Of course, Enoch is there already; see Genesis 5:24.

If Moses is there and Manasseh will be there, what else but amazing grace!

Doesn't this statement sum it up? "There are thousands today who need to learn the same truth that was taught to Nicodemus by the uplifted serpent. They depend on their obedience to the law of God to commend them to His favor. When they are bidden to look to Jesus, and *believe that He saves them solely through His grace,* they exclaim, 'How can these things be?' "[2]

It is my firm belief that if salvation, being a likely candidate for God's eternal kingdom, is a matter of sinlessness, of never breaking the commandments, never disobeying God in any way, being perfectly obedient, reaching the highest point of sanctification, not sinning by commission nor by omission, climbing the Mount Everest of righteousness by sweat and perseverance so that one is equal to Jesus, reaching the goal of godliness and godlikeness, then we all might as well despair. Why? Well, do you know of anyone who's met these standards or reached these goals? Would any of us dare to claim that we have? The only one I know who made this claim and taught others that they could and should make this claim too is now wearing an orange jumpsuit in prison for his "righteous" crimes. If this is your idea of what's required for one to be a likely candidate for the kingdom, when are you planning to meet these requirements? Soon? Just before you die? Shortly before probation closes?

Let me hasten to add some important balance.

- There's no license in grace!
- There's no "my lifestyle doesn't matter" in grace.
- There's no "God doesn't expect me to obey His commandments" in grace.
- Grace has no room for the continuing, willful, I-just-want-to-do-it practice of known sin.
- Grace doesn't coexist with knowingly choosing to disregard light and truth from God's Word.

While grace covers us, forgives us, adopts us into the royal family, makes us heirs with Christ, clothes us with the perfect righteousness of the Savior, it simultaneously gives us a new heart, causes us to walk in God's statutes and judgments, leads us into obedience, produces the fruit of the Spirit, places enmity toward evil in our hearts, and causes us to hunger and thirst for righteousness.

How it all works

I BELIEVE WHO HE IS—the Son of man, the Son of God, the God-man, the Messiah, the Lamb of God who takes away the sin of the world.

I BELIEVE HE lived for me, died for me, was raised for me, intercedes for me now in the presence of the Father, and is coming back for me.

I REPENT AND CONFESS and receive Him as my personal Savior.

I PURPOSE IN MY HEART to love Him, follow Him, and serve Him.

WHEN—NOT *IF*—I FALL, I sorrow, I feel guilty, I hate it, I purpose not to do the same thing again, I turn to 1 John 1:9, "If we confess our sins, He is faithful and just to forgive us our sins," I take Him at His Word, and at some point, victory is mine!

I COME TO HIM, and I keep coming to Him.

I GO ABOUT doing what comes spiritually and rejoice and revel in His saving grace!

BELIEVING ALL OF THE ABOVE moves me, compels me, constrains me to love Him, praise Him, thank Him, obey Him, and serve Him. I do all of this imperfectly and laced with human weakness, but I keep coming, trusting, desiring to be like Him, and doing my best to walk in the Spirit.

BY GRACE, I AM HIS AND HE IS MINE, and I am His candidate for the kingdom!

Please know this:

> Men whom God favored, and to whom He entrusted great responsibilities, were sometimes overcome by temptation and *committed sin*, even as we at the present day strive, waver, and *frequently fall into error* [a euphemism for falling into sin]. Their lives, with all their faults and follies, are open before us, both for our encouragement and warning. *If they had been represented as without fault, we, with our sinful nature, might despair at our own mistakes and failures.* But seeing where others struggled through discouragements like our own, where they fell under temptation as we have done, and yet took heart again and conquered through *the grace of God,* so we too may be overcomers in the strength of Jesus.[3]

Please know this: the devil likes to lead us through our own life gallery and show us all the vivid, ugly, shameful portrayals of past and present that reveal why we are unlikely candidates for the kingdom. All the while, he's hoping we'll get the point, throw in the towel, give it up, quit trying, because "everybody knows" that unlikeliness won't inherit the kingdom.

Please know this: if a man like Samson can be saved, if a man like Manasseh can be saved, if salvation can come quickly and surely to a thief and a jailer and a Samaritan woman, if Brother Serattia can become a likely candidate for the kingdom, then so can I, and so can you!

---

1. Max Lucado, *God Came Near* (Sisters, Ore.: Multnomah Books, 1987), quoted in *The Inspirational Study Bible*, NCV, ed. Max Lucado (Dallas: Word Publishing, 1995), 921, 922; emphasis in original.

2. White, *The Desire of Ages*, 175; emphasis added.

3. White, *Patriarchs and Prophets*, 238; emphasis added.

Questions for Reflection
and Discussion

1. Is the statement that all of us are unlikely candidates for the kingdom offensive? Explain.

2. Do you know someone who *deserves* to be in heaven? If you answered Yes, what about who that person is or what that person has done makes him or her deserving of heaven?

3. Do you think those who just make it into heaven "by their fingernails" will praise God more fervently than those who have been Christians all of their lives? Explain.

4. How do John 3:16; Romans 5:15–21; and 1 John 5:10–12 level the playing field for all those who are saved in the kingdom?

5. Describe the play and interplay of faith and knowledge in a person who's becoming a candidate for the kingdom.

6. In what ways does the fact that we are, indeed, all unlikely candidates for the kingdom affect what we think of other people? How does it affect what we think of really evil people—people such as Hitler, Stalin, child abusers?

7. What is your personal testimony about the grace God has shown you?